*Eugene Raudsepp* is President of Princeton Creative Research, Inc., a firm that specializes in creative problem solving, innovation, and organizational improvement for industry, business, government, and education. He has served as trainer and consultant to several multinational companies, government departments, universities, and management associations. He has written more than 350 articles on business-related subjects, and is the coauthor of *How to Sell New Ideas: Your Company's and Your Own* (Prentice-Hall, 1981).

# HOW TO CREATE NEW IDEAS

For Corporate Profit
and Personal Success

Eugene Raudsepp

A SPECTRUM BOOK

Prentice-Hall, Inc., Englewood Cliffs, N.J. 07632

*Library of Congress Cataloging in Publication Data*

Raudsepp, Eugene.
  How to create new ideas.

  (A Spectrum Book.)
  Includes bibliographical references and index.
  1. Creative ability in business.    2. Success.
I. Title.
HD53.R36     650.1'4     82-365
ISBN 0-13-404517-3     AACR2
ISBN 0-13-404509-2

This Spectrum Book can be made available to businesses
and organizations at a special discount when ordered in large
quantities. For more information, contact:
Prentice-Hall, Inc.
General Book Marketing
Special Sales Division
Englewood Cliffs, N.J. 07632

10  9  8  7  6  5  4  3  2  1

ISBN 0-13-404517-3

ISBN 0-13-404509-2 {PBK.}

Editorial/production supervision
and interior design by Alberta Boddy
Cover design by Velthaus and King
Manufacturing buyer: Cathie Lenard

Prentice-Hall International, Inc., *London*
Prentice-Hall of Australia Pty. Limited, *Sydney*
Prentice-Hall of Canada, Ltd., *Toronto*
Prentice-Hall of India Private Limited, *New Delhi*
Prentice-Hall of Japan, Inc., *Tokyo*
Prentice-Hall of Southeast Asia Pte. Ltd., *Singapore*
Whitehall Books Limited, *Wellington, New Zealand*

# CONTENTS

# PREFACE

Although creativity is one of the most valuable qualities of the human mind, interest in creativity and deliberate attempts to stimulate and encourage it are relatively recent phenomena. These attempts represent one of the most vital turning points of our society for the better —turning away from the rather destructive and disturbing trends in the world and turning to the constructive and creative abilities of the human mind.

It is likely that the current concern about creativity—how to find it, how to nurture it and bring it to full flower, and how to utilize its fruits—stems from the present dearth of significant creativity, the extremely rapid changes we experience in almost every realm of life, and the increasing number of complex and frustrating problems that have come to characterize our present age. There is little doubt that we are facing a future that requires us to be more adaptive and creative in a more active way than we have ever been before. Indeed, we are rapidly moving into a new cultural milieu in which intelligence is no longer enough for solving problems, and in which only the creative individual can cope and flourish.

One of the most eloquent statements reflecting our present need for increasing our capacity for more creativity belongs to the psychologist Carl R. Rogers.

> I maintain that there is a desperate social need for the creative behavior of creative individuals. . . . Many of the serious criticisms of our culture and its trends may best be formulated in terms of a dearth of creativity. Let us state some of these very briefly: In education we tend to turn out conformists, stereotypes, individuals whose education is "completed," rather than freely creative and original thinkers.
>
> In our leisure-time activities, passive entertainment and regimented group action are overwhelmingly predominant, whereas creative activities are much less in evidence. In the sciences, there is an ample supply of technicians, but the number who can creatively formulate fruitful hypotheses and theories is small indeed. In industry, creation is reserved for the few—the manager, the designer, the head of the research department—whereas for the many, life is devoid of original or creative endeavour.
>
> In a time when knowledge, constructive and destructive, is advancing by the most incredible leaps and bounds into a fantastic atomic age, genuinely creative adaptation seems to represent the only possiblity that man can keep abreast of the kaleidoscopic change in his world.*

Beyond the needs of society, another significant development in the creativity movement is the realization of how vital creative thought is to an individual's psychological health. Of all the avenues of personal expression, creativity is the most meaningful, self-fulfilling, and rewarding; it is indispensable for self-realization and for living a full and rich life.

Still another significant discovery—replacing the longstanding idea that creative talent is the province of only a select few—is that most people possess a good deal of creative capacity, although it may be buried under layers and layers of personal and environmental barriers and stiflers. These, however, can be removed, and existing creative potentials and capacities can be improved upon, stimulated, and expanded, even if they have been long dormant or declining.

Creativity and psychological health can be described in the same terms. They are both associated with integration, wholeness, commitment, self-fulfillment, honesty, goal direction, vitality, enthusiasm,

*Carl R. Rogers, *On Becoming a Person.* (Boston: Houghton Mifflin Company, 1961), pp. 347–48.

action, personal involvement, deeper self-realization, higher motivation, and greater self-knowledge.

Not only the future survival of the human species as a whole, but the very *quality* of future human life depends on how well we are able to release and encourage the ability of human beings to think creatively, to reach after new concepts and meanings, to make daring leaps into the unknown, and to find imaginative solutions to the myriad problems facing mankind.

A new workable scheme for the creation of effective ideas requires a wide-angled approach: (1) a thorough understanding of the creative process and the dimensions that go into the creation of an idea, (2) an intimate grasp of the attributes and characteristics of the creative individual, (3) an insight into the blocks and inhibitions to creative thinking and their antidotes, (4) mastery of the various idea-stimulation techniques and strategies, and (5) a thorough understanding of the mechanics of intuitive thinking and fantasy making. It is the purpose of this book to meet these requirements, and its frame of reference has purposely been kept broad, without sacrificing necessary specificity.

Chapter 1 deals with the creative process and focuses on one of the most vital and least understood aspects of the process: the nature of the precognitive germination of the creative idea and the intuitive structuring of the idea while it is emerging from the unconscious. Some of the areas discussed include: misconceptions about the creative process; how ideas occur; why evaluation and judicial attitudes inhibit the creative process; understanding the feelings accompanying the process; how to handle ideas and capture fleeting insights; the vital ability to intimate the "whole" during the process; selectivity during creative problem solving; and the optimum conditions for creative thinking.

Chapter 2 continues the analysis of several aspects of the creative process, concentrating on the attributes of the creative individual in the act of creation. This chapter also explores nineteen of the most vital characteristics and fifteen secondary characteristics necessary for high-level creative functioning.

Chapter 3 provides an in-depth examination of the many emotional, cognitive, perceptual, and environmental blocks and barriers—the unwelcome "dead weights"—that stifle, inhibit, or reduce our creative problem-solving abilities. So many individuals have such a poor capacity to solve problems effectively and bring new ideas into being because they lack insight into the multitude of impediments. This chapter provides useful knowledge and new insights about the ways to avoid or change the factors that work against the flow of ideas.

Chapters 4 and 5 present fourteen successful idea-stimulation techniques and strategies that can magnify and accelerate creative mental processes. These techniques are particularly useful for individuals who feel temporarily stumped in their problem-solving efforts or who seek expanded ways to step up their capacity for producing new ideas.

Chapter 5 describes the Synectics method of formulating new ideas—probably one of the most effective techniques that has been developed to date.

Chapter 6 deals with the vital importance of intuitive thinking in creative problem solving and how the ability to listen to one's hunches can revitalize creativity and imagination. This chapter also describes the latest findings about the modalities and functions of the right and left hemispheres of the brain.

Chapter 7 describes how daydreaming, or fantasy making, can unblock creative energies and open up new, rich potentialities for a creative life style. It shows how to stimulate and harness daydreaming and visualization to sharpen one's goals, and how to gain ready access to the areas of one's imagination that make goal attainment possible.

Chapter 8 presents concrete and practical step-by-step procedures and guidelines that are fundamental to the production of new ideas. It provides specific recommendations on how to define, plan, organize, and structure the creative problem-solving process to ensure maximal creative achievement.

In the area of creativity, even a small increase in efficiency, and a small input of new insights can disproportionately expand the output of new ideas that can yield rich dividends. If this book accomplishes this only, its purpose will be amply fulfilled.

# HOW TO
# CREATE
# NEW IDEAS

# 1

# UNDERSTANDING
# THE CREATIVE PROCESS

One of the most persistent notions about creative ideas is that they come in a flash-like and spontaneous fashion. Perhaps one of the best metaphorical descriptions of the sudden, flash-like birth of the creative idea comes from the contemporary composer, Paul Hindemith. Although written about musical composition, his apt metaphor can be taken to describe equally well how some creative conceptions occur in almost any other field of endeavor.

> We all know the impression of a very heavy flash of lightning in the night. Within a second's time we see a broad landscape, not only in its general outline but with every detail. Although we could never describe each single component of the picture, we feel that not even the smallest leaf of grass escapes our attention. We experience a view, immensely comprehensive and at the same time immensely detailed, that we never could have under normal daylight conditions, and perhaps not during the night either, if our senses were not strained by the extraordinary suddenness of the event. . . . Compositions must be conceived in the same way. If we cannot, in the flash of a single moment, see a composition in its absolute entirety, with every pertinent detail in its proper place, we are not genuine creators.[1]

1

The psychologist L.L. Thurstone also regarded the dramatic, sudden insight, or illumination, as characteristic and critical in creative conception. He considered insight to be the main key to the problem of invention and creative problem solving.

> The moment of insight is the critical moment. The thinking that precedes the moment of insight is different from the thinking that follows that moment. We might define the moment of insight as the main characteristic of work that is called creative. . . . The act is creative if the thinker reaches the solution in a *sudden closure* which necessarily implies some novelty for him.[2]

Although it is true that some creative ideas and solutions to problems undoubtedly owe their existence to sudden, spontaneous insight, a closer study of the creative process indicates that many ideas do not issue from a full-blown, precisely delineated, and firmly structured insight. Neither is the subsequent process of forming and developing an idea always a spontaneous flow of suggestions from the unconscious, reducing the creative individual to a passive transcriber of dictated ideas.

The dramatic instance of a sudden illumination that enables the creative person to perceive the entire novel idea in one fell swoop is in reality a rare and over-publicized phenomenon, grossly exaggerated in the accounts creative individuals themselves have left behind. It is even more unfortunate that this romanticized exaggeration about the sudden complete vision of a new idea has become a firmly rooted notion among our own contemporary investigators and writers on creativity. The perpetuation of this notion can only convince those who fail to experience such apocalyptic visions that they really do not have creative talent, when, in fact, they may have it to a considerable degree. There is little doubt that this notion has dissuaded many budding and promising creative individuals from wholehearted application of their talents. It would, perhaps, be encouraging for them to know that the ideas that have been developed into completed forms are seldom conceived minutely and clearly right in the beginning of the creative process. The creative idea, with only rare exceptions, is initially anything but sharp and sustained, issuing effortlessly into expression. If it were really so, it would reduce the creative process to a noncreative mechanical copying of all the elements that were presented to the creative person in a single, comprehensive insight. As will become apparent, the process of creating is anything but mechanical or passive copying.

## INTUITIVE SENSINGS

A closer scrutiny of the creative process shows that what occurs is a slow, selective structuring of an idea that initially is only imperfectly intimated and that follows the dictates of an intuitive feeling of what belongs and what does not belong, what is proper and what is not. It is a gradual, frequently elusive and groping clarification of a dim and vaguely perceived idea. Perhaps the best way to illustrate this process is through a metaphor.

Let us imagine that we stand at a shore on a foggy day and see a ship sailing in the distance, shrouded by a low, shifting, overhanging fog. Fixing our eyes on the probable course of the ship, we may alternately catch a glimpse of a piece of white sail, or the top of the mast, or the surging prow. The whole thing is never in full view, yet somehow we know that it is there, and eventually we can construct an image of the entire ship. In a similar fashion, in the beginning of the creative process the individual *senses* the total structure of his or her idea, although only a limited number of details of the newly emerging configuration are clearly perceived and delineated. He or she begins by elaborating on the single detail or on a piece of an overall idea. This process of elaboration and shaping of the detail helps other details to emerge. Provided critical judgment is held in abeyance, these details often fall spontaneously into their proper places. Thus the initial idea, rather than being a comprehensive survey of the whole new conception, is often merely a fragmentary particle of the total new idea still to emerge.

Although some intuitive anticipation of the original total concept has to occur in the beginning, it is the process of shaping the elusive, fragmentary insights that actually brings the concept into being. Frequently the shaping of a new creative idea proceeds with unflinching orientation and discrimination, even if awareness of the total meaning of the new idea is not conscious or is only imperfectly so. Not only does the implicit total idea or concept control the entire creative process, but it is impossible for the creative person to impart elements into the evolving idea that do not "jibe" with the commanding *gestalt* of the original conception.

It is the *intuitive sensing,* not an all-embracing insight, that serves as the all-important measure of the elements to be incorporated into the creative product. William J.J. Gordon of Synectics, Inc., has empirically observed intuition *in vivo* with his invention design group. According to him, "intuition is an inner judgment made by the individual about a concept relative to a problem on which he is working. . . . The individual with good intuition is the one who, beyond what could be expected from mere probability alone, repeatedly selects the viewpoint which turns out to lead, for instance, to a great painting or an important invention."[3]

In a vital sense, the creative process can be considered as a movement from the amorphous, dimly and vaguely perceived idea toward a more intelligible structure as the work progresses; from obscure, incommensurable inwardness toward resolved and tangible clarity; from the implicit toward the explicit; from the vaguely intimated toward the known; from the dimly intuited and chaotic toward the reasoned and organized; from the vague meaning toward the clear meaning; from the separately existing paradoxes and contradictory components toward a resolved, unified, and logical structure. The emergence of an idea is gradual, and it is only by virtue of the creative exercise during its formation that the individual finally succeeds in securing the elusive idea.

## SUSPEND CRITICAL JUDGMENT

The acceptance of proposals as they emerge from the unconscious while one is actually working on an idea is a delicate thing. One has to resist the increasing pressure of criticism and judgment that the progressively articulated portions of the idea inevitably elicit. For nothing can inhibit and stifle the creative process more—and on this there is unanimous agreement among all creative individuals and investigators of creativity—than critical judgment at the beginning stages of the creative process. Critical judgment early in the process will inhibit, if it does not completely shut off, the forward propulsions of the emerging idea.

This does not mean that criticism, judgment, and evaluation

have no place in the production of new ideas. On the contrary, these functions serve a very useful purpose. But they serve their purpose at the conclusion of the process, when an open and objective assessment of the idea should be attempted and any pride of paternity suppressed. During the heat of the creative shaping and forming of the idea, however, criticism and judgment must be suspended. The individual should only be aware of the suggestions that emerge from the unconscious. No single item that occurs should be given the center of attention, for this might inhibit further development of the idea. In a sense, the creative person first *feels* an idea, rather than *thinks* or *conceptualizes* it. As Brewster Ghiselin has pointed out, "one must learn to seize and hold them [the initial ideas] without insistence, letting them agitate the mind when and as they may and make their own development, relinquishing them as they fade or fail of effect and taking up others to be cherished without attachment in the same way, shaping the expression of the growing insight critically—that is, consciously and rationally, drawing upon all resources of craft and understanding—*insofar as that may be done without arresting spontaneous development, always preserving the stir of the excited mind* out of which the development issues."[4] (italics mine)

Many creative individuals have indicated how very important it is to be unself-consciously absorbed during the creative process. For example, the composer Aaron Copland offers the following advice, which, in principle, applies to creativity in almost every field: "Inspiration may be a form of superconsciousness, or perhaps of subconsciousness—I would not know: but I am sure that it is the antithesis of self-consciousness. The inspired moment may sometimes be described as a kind of hallucinatory state of mind: one half of the personality emotes and dictates while the other half listens and notates. The half that listens had better look the other way, had better simulate a half attention only, for the half that dictates is easily disgruntled and avenges itself for too close inspection by fading entirely away."[5]

The contemporary poet Richard Wilbur reminds us of Charles Baudelaire's notion that the creative individual must be the "hypnotist and subject at the same time." "This is ticklish business," says Wilbur, and adds, "You have to give the unconscious free play, and at the same time shape the proposals of the unconscious into something that makes daylight sense."

Similarly, the great poet-philosopher Friedrich von Schiller, in an historic letter written in 1788 to a friend who complained of lack of creative power, warned that the intellect should give a wide berth to the incipient ideas in the beginning of the process:

> Apparently it is not good—and indeed it hinders the creative work of the mind—if the intellect examines too closely the ideas already pouring in, as it were, at the gates. Regarded in isolation, an idea may be quite insignificant and venturesome in the extreme, but it may acquire importance from an idea which follows it; perhaps in a certain collocation with other ideas, which may seem equally absurd, it may be capable of furnishing a very serviceable link. The intellect cannot judge all these ideas unless it can retain them, until it has considered them in connection with the other ideas. In the case of a creative mind . . . the intellect has withdrawn its watchers from the gates, and the ideas rush in pell-mell, and only then does it review and inspect the multitude.

James Thurber admonished: "Be a guardian not an usher at the portal of your thought."

Many individuals fail to maximize their creative performance because it is hard for them to entertain the elusive and vague thoughts present during the early stages of the creative process. The indefinite, shapeless, and disorderly state of mind and the incipient, confused excitement that creative activity engenders are something from which they ordinarily flee. Perhaps because of the concrete and practical background of their education and experience, they need a well-defined and clearly blue-printed purpose in view to move with concentration, energy, and courage toward a goal.

A critical attitude, according to several psychologists, seems to be a universally prevalent personality trait; it colors almost all perceptions. The psychiatrist Charles E. Goshen feels that a hypercritical attitude, an overly quick tendency to judge, stems from a need to "always be right" and an extreme sensitivity to criticism. Goshen believes that self-esteem, self-image, and pride hinge largely on success in avoiding criticism. Consequently, as a defense mechanism, such an individual tends to criticize ideas and people with equal fervor. Also, this tendency to be overly critical is usually directed inwardly toward one's own thought processes. Consequently, a critical attitude may well be one of the strongest factors thwarting successful creative problem solving.

One of the primary reasons judicial thinking and creativity make uncomfortable bedfellows is that criticism is based on what is already established, accepted, or proved. Critical judgment must have recourse to past experiences, precedents, and facts—everything that is in the past tense. Being a past-oriented way of thinking, it is essentially opposed to the novel, the untried, and the original. Where creative advance is concerned, however, the past can serve as a guidepost only to a limited degree. Of itself, it is incapable either of bringing the new idea about or of predicting what would happen if it is developed.

The knowledge of what already exists also involves a stereotyped orientation. None of the unexpected and new combinations, contrasts, balances, and configurations of the elements in a creative idea in its formative stage meets the requirements of established laws, facts, or logic. A new creative idea is, of course, based on available knowledge, but it does not issue from it by any direct rational or logical process.

That we have elevated logic and reason to a level where they stifle creative thinking has been pointed out by the psychologist A.R. Wight. He states:

> Perhaps one of the chief forces that inhibit creativity is the emphasis on logic and reason and the lack of respect for intuition. Logic can destroy creativity if demanded or applied too soon, because a creative idea very often is a product of intuition, and the logic supporting it must be developed. Unfortunately, many people in industry have come up through schools where "rule and reason" prevail. They thus feel that nothing is worth consideration that cannot be defended by logic.[6]

Failure to suspend judgment and consider a range of alternatives frequently results in an early commitment to an approach that may contain a "restrictive error" or an "incorrigible strategy." In the perceptual laboratory, for example, subjects who make an early, incorrect interpretation of a picture in an "ambigu-meter" (a device that gradually brings a blurred picture into focus), tend to retain the wrong perception. They fail to "see"—even when the picture has been fully and clearly exposed.

## OPEN-MINDED REFLECTIVENESS

Individuals who are more creative engage in undisciplined, open-minded, and uncritical thinking in the initial stages of the problem-solving process. Gary A. Steiner of the University of Chicago reports,

> Highs [highly creative people] often spend more time in the initial stages of problem formulation, in broad scanning of alternatives. Lows [less creative people] are more apt to "get on with it.". . . For example, in problems divisible into analytic and synthetic stages, highs spend more time on the former—in absolute as well as relative terms. As a result, they may leapfrog lows in the later stages of the solution process. Having disposed of more blind alleys, they are able to make more comprehensive integrations.
>
> Creativity is characterized by a willingness to seek and accept relevant information from any and all sources, to suspend judgment, defer commitment, remain aloof in the face of pressure to take a stand.[7]

Steiner points out, however, that after the initial, open-minded, idea-getting phase and after the examination of many alternatives, creative persons exercise critical judgment. They select the alternative they feel is potentially the best. In the developmental stage an inflexible conviction about the idea's merit takes over. In Steiner's words: "Initially there is an open-minded willingness to pursue leads in any direction, a relaxed and perhaps playful attitude that allows a disorganized, undisciplined approach, to the point of putting the problem aside entirely. But at the point of development and execution, where the selected alternative is pursued, tested, and applied, there is great conviction, even perseverance, perhaps strong personal involvement and dogmatic support of the new way."[8]

Further experimental evidence also indicates that a constructive, rather than a critical or negative approach to ideas produces more creative solutions. The psychologist Ray Hyman conducted several experiments at General Electric and at the University of Oregon. He compared a positive (or constructive) mind set and a negative (or critical) mind set toward both common and uncommon ideas for solutions to a problem. His findings indicated that when subjects review ideas with a constructive set ("What are the good points of these ideas?"), they come up with more creative solutions to the problem than does either the control group (with no instructions) or the group which has been instructed to use a critical set ("What are the weak points?").

Other significant findings of his experiments were that the ideas that were constructively reviewed were often incorporated into the final solution, but the ideas reviewed with a critical mind set were almost always rejected.

Another reason why critical weighing during the creative process should be avoided is that it robs the idea of the value and validity with which it is viewed when it first occurs. More ideas have been prematurely rejected by a stringent evaluative attitude than would be warranted by any inherent weakness or absurdity in them. The longer one can linger with an idea with judgment held in abeyance, the better the chances of capturing all its details and ramifications. Too much elaboration is no problem, because there is always plenty of time later to prune unnecessary details and redundancies from an idea.

## AVOID SELF-CONSCIOUS DELIBERATION

During the heat of creative forming, creative individuals have to entirely abandon themselves to their experience and be keenly aware of only the suggestions that emerge from the unconscious. Consciousness of the familiar has to be blotted out; it is necessary to be in touch with unconscious activity only. As in the procreative embrace, self-consciousness and self-awareness detract from the intensity and fullness of the lovers' communion, so also in the creative process, a lack of total abandon prevents the maintenance of open avenues to the unconscious as a source of ideas.

The intrusion of self-consciousness, the explicit awareness of what one is doing, takes away the necessary ardor and excitement that should attend the creative process, with the consequence that the idea's development may become arrested. Deliberation that is self-conscious can be harmful even during the more conscious and rational development of already secured ideas and insights. Even at this stage a complete absorption in the business at hand is necessary.

Of course, a total loss of consciousness of what is going on or the unconsciousness of the act of creation occur only during a trance-like absorption of the whole personality in the inspirational flow of ideas. The creative act in this case is so intense that the individual creates without knowing that he is creating. But this sort of oblivion to everything, except the suggestions arising from the unconscious matrix, is not the most common experience in creativity. An effortless, unforced spontaneity seldom spans the entire process.

In a sense, evaluation is already at work during the unconscious gestative or formative process of an idea, and it becomes more conscious with the progressive structuring of the idea. But as long as it does not hinder spontaneity or break the rapport with the unconscious, it contributes to the implementation and development of the growing idea.

It is often advisable that these cognitive functions remain submerged and secondary even when the polishing stage of the idea is reached and the pruning of redundant matter becomes the primary concern. For even while polishing, the creative individual has to maintain the grasp of the dominant idea, so as to permit further insights connected with it to emerge into his or her awareness.

It should be also pointed out that one of the chief values of *brainstorming* lies in its encouragement of a nonevaluative atmosphere. Brainstorming is a technique for creating a climate in which the participants are free to express any idea—even a wild or far-fetched one—without fear of provoking negative reactions. In experienced brainstorming groups, "no-holds-barred" thinking and deviating, or divergent, ideas are consciously encouraged, and there is a supportive atmosphere that induces the elaboration of these ideas. The nonevaluative atmosphere also enhances the imaginative exploration of an idea's implications, merits, feasibility of implementation, and range of applications.

## EMOTIONAL CONCOMITANTS
## OF THE CREATIVE PROCESS

Among the observable and introspectively reportable characteristics of the arrival of a new idea is the keen *sense of value* that adheres to it. The idea arrives brimming with positive feeling, giving creative individuals a poignant sense of certainty concerning its relevance to the problem being tackled. At times this pleasant shock of surprise and the sense of profound well-being that the idea induces approach the feeling of rapture.

The positive feeling that infuses the idea undoubtedly lies at the root of many great achievements; still, it is not everything, for the painful process of shaping and forming the idea into a workable thing still lies ahead. Too often it is believed that the idea is, in and of itself, all there is to the creative process. Yet almost everyone has known "idea-persons" who literally shake ideas from their sleeves, but who never amount to much because they fail to work them out into something concrete and practical.

Nevertheless, with most creative people, the emphatic sense of conviction of an idea's vital import and the joy and exaltation that it gives, are largely responsible for putting the entire creative process in motion. Additionally, these positive feelings provide creative people with a reservoir of staying power to conquer every deficiency or temporary block that may occur. It also fills them with a sense of urgency to understand the idea and penetrate into its minutest details. Creative people feel overwhelming pride about their own ideas. This is further demonstrated if, when the finished idea or product does not meet their own approval, they invariably blame their own incomplete skill or knowledge for the failure and see no imperfection in the original concept.

The subjective sense of certainty and conviction that the germinal idea induces in its author is as real as the perception of anything concrete. At the moment the idea occurs, the individual is sure that he or she has seen or grasped the central core or essence of the problem, or that he or she now has the insight for a vital new idea or product. At the moment the idea occurs, no proof is needed that this is the case, although doubt and uncertainty about the validity of the idea may occur later. Nevertheless, the "click" of recognition that an idea represents something significant is seldom betrayed by a truly creative individual, either because of later doubts or because of the overwhelming demands involved in translating the idea into a tangible reality.

The intuitive moment is also frequently accompanied by a *sense of compulsion* that drives the individual to do something with the idea immediately. The idea seems to demand explicit overt action, and this often grows into a full-fledged compulsion if action is delayed or postponed. It invades the consciousness recurrently, no matter what one is doing or thinking, and charges one's thoughts and perceptions, frequently against one's own volition and judgment, in the direction of finding complementary elements or supporting data for the further development of the idea. This compulsion may even, at times, obstruct the emergence of other new ideas if it is not satisfied. Many sterile days or even weeks may pass if the urgency to act on certain compelling ideas is not heeded. At times this seems to have immobilized most of one's available psychic energy. Even while engaged in some other activity, the creative person is often distracted and feels compelled to return to the original idea, even though the time or occasion for considering it is not propitious. Thus the new idea sometimes has the earmarks of obsessive urgency about it.

If one observes the creative process at the highest level—at the genius level—this aspect of compulsive urgency is one of the most striking phenomenon that can be noted. Perhaps the genius-level creative individual should be defined, not so much in terms of a special talent or skill, as by the *intensity* with which he or she formulates conceptions and by the overwhelming and overpowering urgency with which these conceptions surge up into the consciousness, compelling him or her to form and develop them into a tangible reality. With the genius-level individual, there is always a vortex-like intensity, a forceful elan pushing the creative endeavor.

When creative people feel a compulsion to do something with an idea, they may also be overwhelmed by a *sense of possession*—as though the idea originates from some external source rather than from within them, and that their consciousness is acting as only a passive instrument. Ideas frequently amaze creative persons after they are committed to paper. They find that there are many thoughts completely different from those they might have consciously entertained before starting the creative process. Often the finished product appears alien or incomprehensible in the sense that they do not feel fully responsible for it. (Try as one may, and irrespective of the pleasure and pride one may feel, an individual cannot view the finished product with the same ardor of feeling experienced during the act of creation.) The keen feelings of the value of an idea usually abate at the completion of the work. In case of longer creative works, in which interruptions become necessary, it is fascinating to note that the initial idea and the enveloping mood can be reinduced again and again and suffer little or no change in the interim.

## HOW TO HANDLE IDEAS

Creative ideas are often notoriously evanescent and elusive. At the moment the idea appears, the person feels it is impossible to forget it. Yet only moments later, the impression becomes blurred or fades away altogether. If the creative person fails to capture ideas when they occur, fails to fix them in some form for later reference, they frequently vanish and seldom return.

There are creative individuals, however, who prefer not to make a notation of their ideas until they have matured or become more fully structured. They allow glimmerings of an idea to occur to them a number of times, and toy with them repeatedly before making a notation of them. The reason for this is that some ideas take time to mature, and with each successive emergence of them into consciousness, they become more firmly developed. As someone aptly put it, the initial "ideas are more likely to enter the viewfinder of the mind as teasing, wispy, often fleeting images of some sort rather than as carefully crafted full-grown assemblies of memory."

With novice creative individuals, however, it is imperative to fix unexpected ideas in some form as soon as they come. As we have all experienced time and again, some ideas appear to us brimming with importance at the time of their intrusion into our consciousness, yet efforts to recall them often fail. It is therefore imperative that such ideas be committed to paper as soon as they come.

Accomplished creative individuals learn the proper techniques for handling ideas from long practice and frequent disappointments. They learn, for example, that some ideas should be jotted down immediately, as soon as they occur, whereas others should be kept "fluid" and outside conscious focus until the last possible instant, and still others, again, should be dropped back into the unconscious for further development and incubation.

As a general rule, the more complex the idea, the more advisable it is to postpone an early commitment to its main aspects, because there is a real danger of forcing the original idea irretrievably into a restrictive scheme, the limitations of which can impede any subsequent development. On the other hand, it frequently happens that the germinal idea can be completely expressed in one notation, since further gestation would be superfluous or even harmful.

In the final analysis, the dilemma inherent in capturing and developing ideas has to be solved by the individual. Some individuals find that they miss the opportunity to exploit an idea by deferring its notation and by failing to make a definite commitment; others feel that they drain their ideas dry of real novelty by imposing precision on them as soon as they occur. There is, indeed, so much variation in the methods with which creative individuals handle their ideas that they must discover their own happy medium between these extremes to ensure optimum development and utilization of their ideas.

There seems to be a prevalent notion among many investigators of creativity that the initial ideas—those that occur when a person is first faced with finding a solution to a problem—are totally valueless. Although this may be true for attempts to solve relatively unfamiliar problems or those on which no conscious effort has previously been spent, for attempts to solve problems that have been through a period of unconscious cerebration, the first ideas are frequently the best. Consequently, it is advisable to pay closer attention to the first ideas that occur during a productive mood, even though the effortless fashion in which they often appear may make them suspect.

## The Primacy of the Whole

The creative process begins with the *intuitive moment.* This is when creative individuals first grasp the overall essence of the idea that they are about to develop and that might solve the problem. This intimation of the wholeness of the idea comes into being during the creative process through the channel of feeling or intuition. This intuition also directs the shaping of the idea's details during its progressive articulation.

This intimation of the whole has to persevere through every phase of the progressive molding of the idea, until they finally feel that they can give their approval to the outcome. A savoring consummation, a sense of completion, accompanies this act, which in turn signifies that the original concept has been more or less fully exploited.

The intuitive global idea furnishes both the end and the means for achieving the end. It guides the elaborate forming of the idea safely through the shifting chaos of an enormous number of either unconsciously or consciously perceived alternatives and details to its unique terminus. It occasionally happens that many of the elements and details that are first incorporated into a creation may later be dropped or are seen to be irrelevant, and that others may take their place. But this does not argue against the theory that it is the implicit whole that determines what is and what is not admitted into the evolving idea. Only when the individual has firmly grasped the intimated whole can he or she burrow down to the appropriate data in his or her memory bank and assemble the elements that contribute toward the development of the idea. Only then can the creative person introduce proper elaborations to selectively choose past observations and to restructure, combine, and transform the details that go into the development of the idea. All these facets of creative labor are tested by the immediate feeling that the details either belong or do not belong, either contribute or do not contribute to the emerging configuration. This intuitive feeling continues until the individual finds that nothing can be added or changed in this product to improve it.

An emerging concept, as a rule, consists of a series of fragmentary, relatively minor insights before the total import of the idea is realized by the creative individual. When this occurs, the better part of the task may have already been completed and may have been correctly oriented, [so that the import of the more inclusive insight into the original concept does not effect any major revision or reorganization in the already completed portions of the idea]. With many other projects, of course, the wastepaper basket and the littered floor may give silent testimony to numerous arbitrary beginnings, to loose and fumbling directions, or to mounting restlessness and impatience before a satisfactory starting point is trapped.

## DISTRACTIONS IMPAIR CREATIVITY

One reason why the creative process almost invariably produces a severe strain is because the intimation of the implicit idea and its developmental direction must be maintained at all costs throughout many unwelcome distractions (whether external or internal); throughout the fleeting and unexplained momentary inhibitions, irrelevant impulses, sudden fatigue, or flagging interest; throughout moments of self-consciousness and doubts about the idea's real value, and throughout the suddenly remembered obligations and concerns that are the lot of the creative individual in his or her environment.

A pattern quite opposite to the process just outlined occurs when creative individuals feel they can totally abandon themselves to the white heat of a productive mood. They can attend to their work unhampered by the strain of sifting through an excess of consciously perceived alternatives at each successive step in the idea's development. The engrossed creative individuals do whatever their unconscious promptings lead them to, and they ultimately find that the idea has grown effortlessly and spontaneously. As a rule, ideas developed in this fashion need very little revision. All in all, however, this mode of creating, although coveted, either is a relatively rare occurrence or cannot be maintained for too long a period. Constraint, mounting effort, and stress inevitably set in sooner or later.

As tension mounts beyond an optimum point, creative individuals feel forced to spend more and more effort on fewer and fewer results. They find that errors start to pile up and that the direction becomes rambling and confused. This is the time when most creative people quit. Others, the more obstinate ones, stick by their work and either fall back on their richly stocked bag of past methods, or continue consciously to elaborate as much as possible in the remembered key of the initial concept. Numerous rough drafts bear witness to the fact, however, that it is almost impossible for creative individuals to consciously assume conformity to the intimated end of a new idea when the hum of the mood has stopped and when they are no longer in tune with the unconscious. (The firmer one's anticipation of the initial totality, the easier it is to shape its emerging derivatives, ward off random conscious choices, and arrive at a satisfactory creative product.)

## THE END IS ALSO THE MEANS

Many scientists have noted that the intuitive moment indicates the arrival of a possible solution. Albert Einstein, for example, is said to have had the capacity to feel the direction of a possible solution for his problem before he actually knew what the solution was. The psychologist Max Wertheimer, who made a close study of Einstein's thought processes, reports:

> I once told Einstein of my impression that "direction" is an important factor in thought process. To this he said, "Such things were very strongly present. During all those years there was a feeling of direction, of going straight toward something concrete. It is, of course, very hard to express that feeling in words; but it was decidedly the case, and clearly to be distinguished from later considerations about the rational form of the solution. Of course, behind such a direction there is always something logical; but I have it in a kind of survey, in a way visually."[9]

Wertheimer concluded that "scrutiny of Einstein's thought always showed that when a step was taken this happened because it was required." "Quite generally," he adds, "if one knows how Einstein thinks, one knows that any blind and fortuitous procedure is foreign to his mind."[10]

A. Reiser, in his book *Albert Einstein,* comes to a similar conclusion. "Once Einstein has come upon a problem," Reiser writes, "his path toward solution is not a matter of slow, painful stages. He has a definite vision of the possible solution and considers its value and the methods of approaching it."[11] Einstein intuitively sensed what the solution to his problem would be, and he always trusted and acted upon his hunches.

When we closely scrutinize the creative process, it becomes obvious that all the preliminary chaotic gathering of data and facts and the feverish accumulation of materials are only seemingly chaotic and unsystematic. Any person starting research on a particular problem is already under the sway of an intuitive hunch that imputes relevance to the facts he so assiduously collects. No person has ever had a hunch or ever posed a problem while being wholly in the dark about a possible solution and about the data that would be needed to arrive at the solution. If a satisfactory solution is not arrived at, the trouble may lie in the frightful complexity of the problem, rather than in the genuineness of the original hunch.

## SELECTIVITY IN THE CREATIVE PROCESS

The best evidence that there is an intimation of an implicit whole at the intuitive moment is the highly selective activity that occurs throughout the creative process. Selectivity works through the intuitive feeling of moment-by-moment appropriateness and suitability of the details and elements being incorporated into the evolving idea, by guiding their choice and the way they are to be used.

Selectivity operates during the total spectrum of the creative endeavor, starting with the choice of the problem to be worked on. In addition to the compelling preference exhibited toward a problem or idea, there is the selection of specific data to be collected to form the groundwork for solving the problem or developing the idea. Selectivity is also operative in the process of developing the idea: Elements and details that belong are admitted and those felt to be noncontributory are suppressed. Thus selectivity cuts across all the facets of the creative process.

The structure required by the implicitly intimated whole of the novel product is, in the beginning stages, only vaguely felt. Many of the details, their balances, and their correspondences, although tending toward the implicit whole, are not quite consistent or congruent with the intimated whole. Thus they require much restructuring before they conform to the requirements of the implicit configuration. So pervasive and insistent is the established sense of the idea's whole and the unifying pull of its nature, that it imposes the conditions for its realization and inexorably demands the proper transformations and rearrangements. The artist John Ferren has expressed this as follows: "Structure demands a certain quantity and a certain quality of all the elements and insists on it, and it leads you to it or breaks your neck doing it."[12] Ross L. Mooney has remarked on the presence of feeling selectivity in the realm of creative research this way: "The process is held together by feeling. The research man trusts his feeling for telling what belongs and does not belong, what is appropriate, what fits, what is to be taken together. . . . It is the feeling of one's way through, and it will tie in to a thing called appropriateness to fit, to grouping, to clustering."[13]

The feeling or sensing aspect—the affective base in creative activity—cannot be overemphasized, for it constitutes the only yardstick by which the highly selective process during the creative forming works cumulatively toward that essential unifying quality, without which the elements cannot be maintained in their proper places. The creative individual must sense the appropriateness or inappropriateness of every single element added to the developing idea and measure the molding of it by the yardstick of the intuited whole of the idea. He or she must constantly maintain a pervading intuitive sense for the proper balancing of elements and details in order to ensure their rightful place in the orchestration of the whole.

## GRASPING THE ESSENTIALS

The selectivity inherent in the creative process allows the creative individuals to find their way through an enormous number of possibilities and suggestions that sometimes emerge. It enables them to grasp the essentials in chance combinations and helps them to find materials relevant to the central idea among the most disparate and dissimilar elements in the realm of previous experiences. Selectivity acts like a magnet that draws from memory proper facts, data, and impressions, and urges their expression in a form that is, for that particular idea, most fitting in terms of the sensed appropriateness.

The elimination of nonessential or useless ideas during the creative process mainly occurs unconsciously under the influence of the original conception. This elimination is implicit, because most of the useless combinations seldom emerge into the consciousness or become available to analytic recognition. If some of them should emerge, they may influence the creative activity by temporarily blocking the emergence of the proper elements.

The famous French mathematician Henri Poincaré first indicated that the elimination of inessential elements occurs mainly in the unconscious. "It is certain that the combinations which present themselves to the mind in a kind of sudden illumination after a somewhat prolonged period of unconscious work are generally useful and fruitful combinations, which appear to be the result of a preliminary sifting. But how can we explain the fact that, of the thousand products of our unconscious activity, some are invited to cross the threshold, while others remain outside? Is it mere chance that gives them this privilege? Evidently not." Poincaré then continues in a more explicit vein by stating that "the sterile combinations do not even present themselves to the mind of the inventor. Never in the field of his consciousness do combinations appear that are not really useful, except some that he rejects but which have to some extent the characteristics of useful combinations."[14]

Poincaré also recognized what most highly creative individuals have noticed, namely, that their unconscious has a discerning, discriminating power that can effect correct choices even when the conscious or rational reasoning has given up the battle as lost.

Not only is there the crowding out of many elements and details that have no relationship with the idea, but also the establishment of a permissive condition for combinations and syntheses to occur. It often happens that after the new idea has become more explicit, it assumes the characteristics of an *idée fixe*. This enables the creative thinker to gather impressions, data, facts, and information in support of the development of the idea in the most unlikely realms of knowledge and experience. Phenomena that did not originally appear to be related to the creative individual's preoccupation now fall under the beam of the fixed idea and are interpreted in its light. The individual's perceptions become selectively attuned to notice and register things that seem to add, verify, or confirm the idea. Also present is an increased ability to organize and combine these contributory impressions so that they will fit into the central theme of the idea.


## OPTIMUM CONDITIONS
## FOR CREATIVE THINKING

The appearance of new ideas cannot easily be foretold, except, perhaps, by a peculiar feeling of restlessness just before the one appears, and it is quite impossible to induce ideas at will. Creative ideas are not under one's voluntary control. As a consequence, they cannot be governed by planning, schedules, or sheer enforcement. Johann Wolfgang von Goethe, for example, attributed his sixty years of toil with *Faust* to the detrimental and barren efforts of his will. The will reigns over the already established order of consciousness; it does not have the power to induce a flood of novelty from the unconscious, hences the sterile periods and dark days known to all creative individuals.

But once the creative current runs strong and the organic development of the idea is underway, one can assume an attitude that resembles the will and that helps to maintain the creative heat at a desirable intensity. This attitude is a wish, a challenging urge on the part of the creative individual to give his or her utmost while submitting to the workings of the creative act. Many creative individuals want to transcend their past performances and to give their best to every new occasion of problem solving, in order to achieve more than they have before. This urgent wish toward a fuller and richer self-realization helps the creative individual to sustain the intensity of the creative mood and to keep the avenues to the unconscious free from internal and external interruptions, as well as from the established habit patterns of consciousness.


## THE BEST TIME FOR CREATING

Although it is impossible to induce creative ideas at will, there are, nevertheless, certain propitious conditions that help to prompt ideas. These conditions help stimulate the potent unconscious matrix from which novel ideas spring forth. For example, nighttime—when the world sleeps and the wearisome hustle of the day has exhausted itself—is the time of day for innumerable individuals that is most conducive to a creative mood and to a creatively detached condition. It is at night when many creative individuals begin to anticipate, as one creative person so aptly put it, "a blind date with their deeper selves." Daytime, on the other hand, with its predominantly practical orientation, its bustling activity, and its incessant noise, can act as a blockage to creative ideas and prevent their flow from the unconscious. Nighttime, with its all-pervading peace and the inscrutable mystery of darkness, brings to many creative individuals a spiritual rapport and identification with nature, or a sense of cosmic isolation that is conducive to the arousal of a creative mood.

There are individuals, of course, who prefer the early morning hours—the freshness of a newborn day—for their creative labors. Others need high-powered activity around them in order to release their ideas. They have to escape into the whirlwind of organizational hustle and depend on its restless activity for the necessary stimulus of productive ideas. In this case, the knack of closing out the external world at will and of being able to detach themselves instantaneously and whenever necessary is an essential ability in their repertoire.

It must be noted that the ability to become inwardly isolated at will is not necessarily conditioned on outward isolation, and many creative individuals can tune in on their private selves in the noisiest environments. The ability to inwardly isolate oneself from one's immediate environmental activity and obligations is, however, the primary requirement for significant creative work. Without such detachment, one cannot fully exploit his or her creative ideas. In fact, periods of inward detachment from the encumbrances of environment can be more productive than hours of merely physical isolation.

## THE POWER OF ECCENTRIC RITUALS

Many of the idiosyncracies and peculiarities of creative individuals have been the delight of biographers, providing an endless source of anecdotal material. These idiosyncracies have often been the peculiar ways they evoke and maintain the creative mood.

Claude Debussy, for example, used to gaze at the river Seine and the playful golden reflections of the setting sun on its waves to establish an atmosphere for composing. Johann von Schiller kept rotten apples in his desk drawer. Their aroma helped him to evoke a mood for creative work. Feodor M. Dostoevsky found that he could best brood and dream up his immortal stories and characters while pen-drawing and doodling.

It seems that there is hardly a creative individual who does not have a special habit, eccentricity, or ritual for provoking free-floating concentration and an uncensored alertness to all the implications and developments of a novel idea. Such idiosyncracies also seem necessary for keeping the overactive thought patterns of consciousness in abeyance and for shutting out all other distractions. By anchoring oneself to only one distraction, such as smoking, biting the end of a pencil, or scratching one's forehead, outward distractions are muted or recede into nothingness. This is essential, for a shrill ringing of the telephone in the next room, a conversation down the hall, a rumbling stomach, or some other momentary bodily discomfiture could act as a pinprick to shatter the creative mood. By channeling the distraction into one ritual or habit, all other distractions lose their disrupting power.

Many creative individuals pace the floor endlessly and biographies are replete with instances of ideas occurring to creative individuals when they were walking, hiking, or traveling. That physical motion animates and augments the flow of images and ideas and that our legs are the *wheels of thought* have been known to creative workers throughout the ages.

When creative individuals prefer to work and what habits they develop to concentrate most effectively cannot be understood in terms of any cause-and-effect relationships. There is so much variation in the habits and preferred times for working that it can safely be concluded that the only optimum times and conditions for producing novel ideas are when the creative individual attains an uncluttered rapport with his or her unconscious and feels free from the practical demands of the environment. Another condition is that the creative person should also be free from the stereotypical orientation of his or her own noncreative periods of working and living and from the conservative, established ways of thinking that crowd the consciousness during these periods. These conditions are illustrated by the frequent claims that the most valued ideas of creative individuals occur to them during passive, relaxed, or even fatigued states.

## STIMULATION
## FROM INSIGNIFICANT INCIDENTS

The creative mood may seize the individual without any detectable reason or stimulus. It apparently can be catalyzed by many insignificant and wayward incidents. Since one of the salient characteristics of intuitive moments is that they are not under voluntary control, often occurring, therefore, without warning, creative ideas may and do appear at any hour and under the strangest of circumstances.

For example, there is a story about Antonio Vivaldi being overcome by inspiration while celebrating Mass. As soon as the "divine afflatus" had struck him, he rushed away from the altar into the sacristy, where he wrote down his theme. It was only after he had carefully marked down the melody and assured himself of its retention that he returned to the altar to resume the Mass. Needless to say, the officials of the church, ignorant of the wayward surprises of the creative process, summarily dismissed him from his office.

Another incident that has been reported about Sir Isaac Newton was that during the course of a dinner he was giving to his guests, he left the table to get some wine from the cellar. On his way, he was overcome by an idea, forgot his errand and company, and was soon hard at work in his study.

Many seasoned creative individuals have an unreasoned, intuitive sense for the *preparatory* cues and the external conditions that are necessary for evoking a creative mood. Although it is impossible to summon creative ideas at will, many creative individuals have mastered the art of exposing themselves to stimuli that trigger the creative mood. Experience eventually shows every creative person which environmental conditions are propitious for receptive concentration.

There are many stimuli that act as catalytic agents and induce such a mood. We all know that an interesting lecture, a visit with a friend, an overheard perceptive remark, a hike in the freedom of nature—as a matter of fact, any stimulating event that upsets "the needle in the groove"—may put us in a proper mood for creative work. For the painter, this may be the smell of paints or turpentine; for the composer, the sound of distant music; for the writer, a stimulating exchange of ideas; for the scientist or engineer, the sight of laboratory equipment or some brand-new tools. These are cues that are more or less directly associated with a creative individual's particular work, but not with the specific problem that is later solved or with the idea that is later developed.

Appreciators and spectators of art also react to preparatory cues. Thus the sound of musicians tuning their instruments before a performance of an opera or a concert serves to put the audience into a receptive state of mind; in museums and art galleries the hushed silence, the appreciative cocking of heads, and the pensive stance of posture may be sufficient to engender the same kind of attitude: a detachment, however transitory, from personal cares and preoccupations.

There are, on the other hand, long stretches of barren periods in every creative individual's life. It might be safe to say that, for every creative worker who is periodically successful in solving problems, there are several who go through varying degrees of barren sterility and who only manage an occasional glimpse of the tail end of an evanescent mood. To some perhaps less integrated individuals, there are periods when the incipient mood for creative activity serves to arouse all kinds of conflicts instead of healing ideas, with the result that they lapse and remain in a state of indolence, lassitude, and apathy, and find numerous excuses to postpone creative work, sometimes for months or even years. Others again desperately pine for the return of a creative mood, but are unable to rouse the power from its slumbers. To be sure, there may be relatively long periods in every creative individual's life when, for one reason or other, the creative fountain has run dry and one can only imitate old achievements. But creative people usually manage to survive these periods of sterility and continue to grow with the renascence of their productive powers. Luckily, as the writer Colin Wilson has suggested, "creative energy tends to be self-renewing, and to produce its own chain reaction of health and further effort."[15]

There are also a large number of creative individuals who work daily, irrespective of the presence of a driving inspiration. They show an amazing amount of patience and fortitude in mastering their disinclinations to work. While the amount and quality of their legacy to the creative arsenal may not in any way exceed the legacy of those creative individuals who evidence no such routine in their output, at least they are spared the pain and humiliation of barrenness.

Most creative individuals claim that they benefit from regular work habits. They know how to regulate the preparation or intake of fresh information, experiences, and impressions; they know that they have to earmark time for the digestion or incubation processes; they observe how long it takes for novel insights to emerge and how long it takes to elaborate them into viability. The creative individual is likely to show maximum efficiency in creative output when he or she adheres to an individual rhythm inherent in these phases. Frequent violation of any of them by undue haste or tardiness can retard creative efficiency.

# REFERENCES

[1] Paul Hindemith, *A Composer's World.* (Cambridge, Mass.: Harvard University Press, 1952), p. 60.

[2] L.L. Thurstone, "Creative Talent," *Reports from the Psychometric Laboratory*, no. 61, Chicago: University of Chicago, 1950, p. 3.

[3] William J.J. Gordon, *Synectics.* (New York: Harper & Brothers, 1961), p. 156.

[4] Brewster Ghiselin, *The Creative Process.* (Berkeley, Ca.: University of California Press, 1952), p. 15.

[5] Aaron Copland, *Music and Imagination.* (Cambridge, Mass.: Harvard University Press, 1952), p. 42.

[6] A.R. Wight, "What Does Industry Want—Creativity?" (unpublished paper), p. 27.

[7] Gary A. Steiner, ed., *The Creative Organization.* (Chicago: The University of Chicago Press, 1965), p. 10.

[8] Ibid., p. 15.

[9] Max Wertheimer, *Productive Thinking.* (New York: Harper & Brothers Publishers, Inc., 1945), p. 184.

[10] Ibid., p. 188.

[11] A. Reiser, *Albert Einstein.* (London: Thornton Butterworth Ltd., 1931), pp. 116–17.

[12] John Ferren, in *The Nature of Creative Thinking*, Industrial Research Institute, p. 62.

[13] Ross L. Mooney, "Groundwork for Creative Research," *The American Psychologist*, 9, no. 9, (Sept. 1954), 544.

[14] Henri Poincaré, *Science and Method.* (Nashville, Tenn.: Thomas Nelson, Inc., 1914), p. 383.

[15] Colin Wilson, *New Pathways in Psychology.* (New York: Taplinger Publishing Co., 1972), p. 172.

# 2

# CREATIVE PEOPLE

Creative people share many distinct attributes, or characteristics, by which they can be identified and which significantly differentiate them from people who are less creative or even noncreative.

Before describing the attributes in detail, it should be pointed out that no one individual could hope to possess all of these to the same high degree. Rather, the descriptions should be taken as a composite profile of the "ideal" creative individual. There are many gradations in the attributes and skills creative people possess. However, every creative individual has at least some measure of these attributes in order to earn the appellation "creative." Also, certain assemblies or combinations of ideational dexterity frequently compensate for many attributes that are less developed or have fallen into disuse.

Another thing that must be pointed out is that no attempt is made in this chapter to divide or classify these attributes into the customary cognitive, affective, and conative groupings. The reason for this is that the attributes of creativity are not self-contained units, but they overlap and merge into one another, partaking of the affective, the cognitive, and the conative. It would be idle and meaningless to attempt to draw sharp lines between them. One cannot divide a personality into characteristics the way bread can be sliced into pieces. The slices of bread add up to the complete loaf, but personality characteristics fail to add up to the total personality. It is only to facilitate analysis and description that the characteristics are treated here as discrete entities.

What is the value of gaining insight into the attributes of the creative personality? Since people often learn by imitation, a person can substantially increase his or her creative capacities and performance by deliberately cultivating those characteristics it is felt he or she does not possess to a sufficient degree or by "dusting off" those that have fallen into disuse. The reader would be well advised to study these characteristics closely, so they can become part and parcel of his or her personality make-up.

## SENSITIVITY TO PROBLEMS

The philosopher John Dewey was one of the first to note that creativity does not start with facts, theories, or hypotheses, but with a *problematic situation*. He felt that sensitivity and the ability to envisage and formulate the right problem are crucial to effective problem solving.

Creative persons have keen powers of observation and an unusual ability to perceive and notice problems, situations, and challenges that have escaped the attention of others. This is because of their greater sensitivity to the unusual, the odd, or the promising aspects of situations—hidden opportunities often overlooked by other individuals. Exceptional, incongruous, paradoxical or unusual happenings and situations can snap creative people to instant attention; they become the grist for the mill of their minds. Because of a questioning approach to almost everything they encounter, creative people don't take the obvious for granted. Rather, they deliberately place problems in new and different perspectives in order to approach solutions from unique vantage points. In addition to this capacity to note and arrest the unusual or different and to see gaps and unrealized potentials in situations is an equally highly developed ability to see resemblances, similarities, and analogies among a multitude of different experiences.

Perhaps because creative people have a greater sensitivity to self, to others, and to sensory stimuli from the outside world, they tend to be dissatisfied with things as they are and to be eager to improve them. Hence they are constantly either seeking and finding challenging problems to solve. They are like the proverbial philosopher with a "thorn in his flesh," in that they are perpetually disturbed by something. For creative people there is hardly a situation entirely free of problems, but this does not cause them frustration and worry. On the contrary, they welcome the challenge of problems and the state of "happy" dissatisfaction with the status quo. They know that creativity grows, as the poet A.E.Houseman speculated, out of irritation like a pearl secreted from the friction-generating particle of sand in the oyster's shell.

## FLUENCY

In addition to sensitivity, two other attributes crucially vital for creative problem solving are *fluency* and *flexibility*.

Creative individuals have the ability to generate a large number of ideas when confronting a problem or seeking improvements. They can scan more alternative thoughts, ride the wave of different associative currents, and think of more ideas in a given span of time than do persons who are less creative. Capable of tapping a tropical imagination and producing ideas in volume, they stand a better chance of selecting and developing significant ideas.

Fluency can be demonstrated by a simple test that was developed by the psychologist J.P. Guilford.[1] One can ask people to list as many uses as they can think of for some common object, such as, for example, a red brick. If they list a large number of uses all in one class or category, such as construction or adornment, they show fluency. If, in addition, they list a number of uses that range over several categories (there are over sixteen such categories in the case of a red brick), they show not only fluency but flexibility as well.

It must be pointed out that fluency of ideas and spontaneous expressiveness can be considerably enhanced if one learns to deliberately restrain or suppress critical judgment and evaluation of ideas as they occur—until one has marshaled all the ideas one is capable of. An overdeveloped or too early critical attitude during the creative process can thoroughly inhibit fluency and the forward propulsion of ideas.

The educator Leif Fearn explains fluency this way:

> Fluency is the identification and isolation of knowns. It is rather like rummaging through one's space to make conscious all the possibilities, no matter how remote, that surround a question or problem. . . . One characteristic of fluent behavior is its chaining effect where, given the freedom to brainstorm, some ideas trigger other ideas that may have remained obscure had the production of ideas been limited. . . . Fluent behavior has no judgment component because it has nothing to do with "good," "feasible," or "appropriate" ideas. It is purely a searching behavior where the objective is to make conscious as much data as possible.[2]

While there is little doubt that people who want to increase their creativity in problem solving should be willing to try a wide variety of wild shots in the dark, so to speak, and list a wealth of notions and ideas, it must not be overlooked that fluency constitutes just the initial stage of the creative process. Fluency has to be strongly coupled with, first, the selectivity to choose the most fundamental aspects of the problem and, second, the ability to identify which of the many alternatives are the best for solving the problem. Easy rhetoric and ebullient fantasy that are not guided by these two principles do not guarantee adeptness in creative problem solving.

## FLEXIBILITY

Creative persons are flexible in their thinking. They are able to choose and explore a wide variety of approaches to a problem, without losing sight of the overall goal or purpose. During problem solving, if new developments or changed circumstances demand, creative people can easily drop one line of thought or an unworkable approach and take up another. They show resourcefulness in their ability to shift gears, to discard one frame of reference for another, to change perspective, to modify approaches, and to adapt quickly to new developments or requirements. They constantly ask themselves, "What else?" or "What would happen if I viewed the problem from a different angle?"

The scientist James H. Austin distinguishes between two kinds of flexibility: "One is the tendency to shift from one category of meaning to another; the second is loose and unstructured meandering of attention, a readiness to free associate, to daydream, to unleash one's thoughts into broad unclassified paths only tangentially related either to the starting point or to each other." Austin feels that this kind of flexibility correlates with the rapid production of original ideas.[3]

The associative links between ideas and their components that creative people form during problem solving are loose, fluid, and capable of being dissociated and then reassembled into new patterns. They have no obsessive need to arrive at a closure by prematurely categorizing and structuring any of the elements. They rather prefer to consider, test, and weigh the many configurations before deciding on one to solve a problem. Able to perceive a problem from different viewpoints, creative people can "bombard" it with a variety of possible solutions. They are free from what is termed "hardening of caretories."

Hardening of categories is frequently the result of overfamiliarity with certain objects. As the late professor John E. Arnold of Stanford University put it: "We see a pencil as only a writing instrument, we never see it as a tool for propping open a window, or as fuel for a fire, or as a means of defending ourselves in an attack. A pencil is a pencil. It is not a combination of graphite, wood, brass, and rubber, each of which have multiple properties and multiple uses.[4]

## ORIGINALITY

Creative people display originality in their thinking. Since their thought processes are not jammed up with stereotypes, they can reach out beyond the ordinary or commonplace and can think of more unusual and unique solutions to problems. Originality expresses itself also in the ability to dissect firmly structured and established systems, to dissolve existing syntheses, and to use elements and concepts beyond the limits they possess in their primary contexts in order to create a new combination or a new system of relationships.

In addition to this ability to fragment and differentiate, the creative person is also able to find unity in diversity, to see unexpected relationships and kinships, similarities, likenesses, and connections between things, experiences, and phenomena that to the noncreative person evidence no relationship whatsoever—until pointed out.

Creative people are always in quest of the new, always ready to see something unexpected, novel, and fresh in all experiences. Generous toward unusual ideas, whether they be their own or another's, creative people are openminded sometimes to the point of gullibility in accepting bizarre or even crackpot ideas. They are apt to toy with such notions quite seriously before relegating them to the wastebasket as useless or invalid. New perspectives, novel ideas, and venturesome conceptions provide an endless source of exercise for the creative mind.

Originality feeds on change. It is for this reason that many creative individuals—through travel and immersion in new happenings—perpetually seek to reexperience, time and again, the quality of freshness and the feeling of novelty.


## CURIOSITY


Creativity is, in an important sense, contingent upon the preservation of curiosity and the sense of wonder that are so apparent in youth and so conspicuously absent in many grownups. The educational and developmental processes most people go through, while ostensibly preparing them for the responsibilities of adulthood, nevertheless manage to conventionalize them to a point when lively curiosity and wonder almost cease to exist. In addition or perhaps as a consequence of this, many adults have a deep distrust of originality, imagination, and fantasy making. They often show this by their spontaneous tendency to criticize or dismiss thoughts that cannot be defended by facts or logic. There is little doubt that this closed mindedness has conditioned much of our society with a timid cautiousness that prevents many valuable ideas from taking root.

Children have a keen and intense awareness of their environment. They have a ready feeling of curiosity toward everything they touch or come in contact with, a precious propulsion toward seeking understanding, toward piercing the mystery they sense in everything they perceive.

The rapt sense of children's wonder, the avid interest in the minutest details of their surroundings, and, indeed, their sheer poetic intensitiy of living disappear sooner than all the other characteristics of childhood. Only the truly creative individual manages to retain this early sense of curiosity. It is this lively attitude of curiosity and inquiry that enables the creative person to constantly enrich and add to his or her store of information and experience.

Another noteworthy characteristic of creative people is their wide-awake attitude of inquiry. It invariably extends far beyond the confines of their specialization or main line of work. Their wide spectrum of interest embraces many related and unrelated areas and fields. They can get excited about almost any problem or phenomenon that puzzles or mystifies. Many things taken for granted by others are a challenge for creative people. In this sense they are intellectually restless; not satisfied with what is accepted, established, or known; constantly wondering how things could or might be; and always ready to consider and visualize new possibilities. They feel that it is necessary to improve upon, or add to, existing realities.

## OPENNESS TO FEELINGS
## AND THE UNCONSCIOUS

Creative people have more energy, are more impulsive, and are more responsive to emotions and feelings than less creative people. Since they are more in touch with and open to their internal processes, they have better access to buried materials in the unconscious. Or, to put it differently, their ability to minimize internal defenses and inhibitions and their relative lack of defensive distortions and repressions enable them to have a more direct and uncluttered pipeline to the real wellspring of ideas—the unconscious.

According to the psychologist Abraham H. Maslow, the really creative person is one who accepts his or her essentially *androgynous* character: "This is the person who can live with his unconscious; live with, let's say, his childishness, his fantasy, his imagination, his wish fulfillment, his femininity, his poetic quality, his crazy quality. He is the person, as one psychoanalyst said in a nice phrase, 'who can regress in the service of the ego.' This is voluntary regression. This person is the one who has that kind of creativeness at his disposal, readily available, that I think we're interested in."[5] According to Maslow's theory, there are two distinct kinds of creativity: primary and secondary. Primary creativity emerges from the unconscious; it is the source of new discoveries, novelties, and ideas that depart from what exists at the moment; it is common and universal to all people; it is found in healthy children; it comes from those who are able to play, dream, laugh, and loaf; it comes from those who can be spontaneous and more open to unconscious promptings and impulses; it is present in those who accept their softness and some weakness; and it is found more among individuals who have a keen interest in the artistic and aesthetic fields.

On the other hand, secondary creativity comes primarily from the conscious; it comes from rigid, constricted people who are afraid of their unconscious and who are cautious and careful in everything they do; it comes from those who can't play very well and who excessively control their emotions; it is characteristic of those individuals who demand a high degree of order in their lives and who dislike poetry and other types of emotional expression; it is present in those who drown their childishness, who are afraid of their softness and who repress all weakness.

According to Maslow, the healthy creative person is not one who exclusively uses either the primary or the secondary processes, but one who has managed a fusion or synthesis of the primary and the secondary processes, of the conscious and the unconscious, of the deeper self and the conscious self.

Since creative people put great trust in their feelings and intuitive sensings, they are readily able to utilize them as guides during the creative process of finding unique solutions to problems. When judging the relevance of ideas that develop during the process, the creative person measures their appropriateness or pertinence by their feeling of fitness and harmony.

## MOTIVATION

Basic to creative achievement is the strong desire to create. The creative person derives great satisfaction from creative activities and is keenly interested in his or her chosen work and the materials he or she works with. The inevitable difficulties do not discourage creative people. They welcome problems as personal challenges and look forward to the time when they can grapple with them. They assume an optimistic stance vis-à-vis their problems, and feel, like Pogo, that they are "confronted with insurmountable opportunities."

Creative people like to pursue problems that are intrinsically of high interest and that are governed and guided more by inner stimulus than by outer demand. They create not because someone wants them to create, but because they must. In a sense, they are at the mercy of their own values and motivations and can operate with maximum effectiveness when dealing with problems that have the strongest emotional affinity to personal interests.

Highly creative individuals are frequently haunted by problems and cannot let go of them. Anyone who observes the creative person at work is impressed by the full absorption and vigorous concentration that infuses such activity. This strong sense of purpose and commitment and the intensity with which he or she encounters problems show strong ego-involvement. This ego-involvement is responsible for the unusual staying power that the creative individual exhibits.

Creative people are ready to engage in meaningful problem solving purely for the satisfaction that it provides, even when no other rewards lie ahead. This explains why they go to great lengths to find problems that pertain mostly to personal interests and that are a real challenge to all of their capacities. Their motives are more internal and goal-centered than competitive, and they are not unduly influenced by what others may be expecting.

The chosen life's work of creative people is their most important avenue for fulfillment. Creative people are fully dedicated to what they are doing; this dedication provides a sense of joy. Unlike the majority of human beings, they are not preoccupied with the pursuit of happiness, rather, they find happiness in the pursuit of creative activities.


## FREEDOM FROM FEAR OF FAILURE


Because the career orientation of most people is governed by the premise of success, the specter of failure looms large. In the risk-taking enterprise of creativity, however, failures do sometimes occur. No new ground under exploration is completely secure under foot. One needs to respond positively to the risk and the challenge of exploring new frontiers. As James H. Austin puts it: "Creativity involves taking one step after another into pitch darkness—not a fussy rearranging of familiar furniture in a flood-lighted room."[6] The attitude that is requisite for risk-taking is well expressed by the American painter Albert Pinkham Ryder: "Have you ever seen an inchworm crawl up a leaf or twig and there, clinging to the very end, revolve in the air feeling for something to reach? That's like me. I'm trying to find something out there beyond the place I have a footing."[7]

Fear of failure prevents many individuals from daring anything really creative, especially when the element of risk-taking is considerable. Their attitude of caution is dictated by fear of the consequences of failure, which casts such a fearful shadow on them because of their self-induced heavy responsibility for accurate judgment and their pride in the ability to operate and plan successfully. Although the ability to exercise sound judgment is valuable, it nevertheless qualifies their willingness to risk the kind of leap into the unknown that is involved in genuine creative advances.

Actually, failure should be regarded as a "learning situation"— a situation in which new or improved ideas may arise. Almost every area of development has had its history of failures before it ultimately led to success. In reality, the greatest failure is not to attempt a new idea at all.

## PERSISTENCE AND CONCENTRATION

An enormous capacity for taking pains, a dogged persistence in the face of difficulties and frustrations, and a vast amount of sheer arduous work are some of the other outstanding attributes that mark the creative person. These qualities stand out in their biographies, and they are also the ones they emphasize most when counseling others with creative aspirations.

The popular notion that the creative individual relies mainly on effortless inspiration and unenforced spontaneity is still a widespread misconception. It is not fully realized that creative achievement requires a hard core of self-discipline and arduous, unceasing application. It also requires confidence, the maintenance of morale, and long-lasting pervasive excitement to stubbornly resist premature discouragement in the face of difficulties and temporary failures. Although creative persons occasionally experience failure, they are not downed, crushed, or maimed by it. They feel that unfavorable conditions are only temporary and that they will eventually become favorable when met with determination to persist and to keep on going. As Einstein once remarked, "I think and think, for months, for years. Ninety-nine times the conclusion is false. The hundredth time I am right."

From talking to highly creative individuals, it becomes clear that the majority of them do not know what a mere eight-hour workday means. Their preoccupation with problems is incessant. Occasionally they may have moments in their work that are crowned with joy, when, for example, they find that ideas start flowing again after they have surmounted a disrupting hitch. But frequently the intense struggle with problems does not yield immediate solutions. As someone put it: "Creativity can be, and often is, a savage experience demanding hard work and the willingness to live with a task to a self-defined conclusion."

Many creative individuals have shown tremendous concentration and persistence. Zona Gale, the Pulitzer Prize-winner, labored as an unknown writer for many years, but continued to persist and persevere in her occupation almost every night, while working to support herself during the day. The painter Mary Cassatt showed enormous abilities to concentrate and persevere even when she was sick and advanced in years. Marie Curie was able to devote her total concentration upon the work she was doing in her laboratory, day in and day out. Rosalyn Yalow, a Nobel Prize-winner in medicine, frequently worked up to 100 hours a week, not because she had to, but because she wanted to.

Creation is preceded by hard thinking, prolonged reflection, and concentrated hard work. There is a continuous assimilation of new knowledge and experiences, a continuous pondering on the causes of the difficulties that are regularly met with, and a sorting out of hunches and ideas that flash across the firmament of consciousness. It is apparent that all this takes time and a willingness to experience and accept the many agonies along the route. Occasionally, they may even be felt to be excessive. It is almost proverbial how many creative individuals have threatened to quit their work for good, especially when their wastepaper baskets were overflowing with discarded worksheets. At times of insoluble snags and feelings of helplessness, even the prospect of digging ditches looks like an easy way out. But the next day they are back, probing and attacking problems, determined to complete what is unfinished.

Quite often in the beginning stages of creative problem solving, conscious efforts are abortive and useless, and creative individuals have testified of many times they had to give up their efforts temporarily and of how many of their initial attempts ended in failure before a valid solution or idea emerged. Still, all these apparently futile initial efforts are not as wasted as they seem, but they serve to activate the unconscious processes of cerebration and incubation. Without preparatory work, the unconscious can be notoriously unproductive.

It is true that some creative persons rely more deliberately on the gestative process of the unconscious to complete the ideas for them. With most creative individuals, however, a dogged and intense preliminary effort—a lot of exhausting spadework—constitutes the necessary prelude to original production. The capacity for original work grows out of long training, constant application, and unflagging persistence.

Since, in the course of creative work, a lessening of persistence frequently occurs—sometimes due to repeated failures, at other times to lessening of interest—it serves well to learn to cope with this reaction. Discomfort with persistence or a feeling of flagging interest are often an indication of a need to get away from a problem and to relax for awhile. Creative individuals often find that they can relax by working on another challenging problem. Many of them say that they function best when involved in several undertakings simultaneously, each at a different stage of development, each affording an opportunity to relax when interest or ability to persist in working at another problem fails.

The creative process also requires concentration and continuous thinking until the creative person becomes oblivious to his or her surroundings. During the creative process he or she maintains an uninterrupted rapport with the unconscious and formulates the emerging proposals into something that makes sense. This requires disciplined concentration. The philosopher Richard Guggenheimer explains it this way:

> A great disciplinary effort is required for most productive minds before they reach a stage where they are able to swiftly launch themselves into completely spontaneous absorption in the creative business at hand. A

thousand and one diverting thoughts must be suppressed; the mind must brush aside myriad temptations to amble here and there along the enticing byways of casual thinking. It must become totally involved in the mounting wave of its deep intent. The principal labor is getting the wave started; most of us splash about in our thinking and mistake the ripples of our noisy commotion for real movement.[8]

Of course, when there is a complete and wholehearted absorption in the business at hand, the activity itself helps the process along. Suggestions on how to proceed occur spontaneously. One no longer has to use energy to force one's own mind to concentrate on the problem. Great disciplinary effort is invariably required, however, at the beginning stages of the problem-solving process. At these stages, many extraneous thoughts must be discarded or suppressed in order to plug into the creative current.

## BACKGROUND
## OF FUNDAMENTAL KNOWLEDGE

In spite of the increasing contemporary trend toward specialization in almost every occupation and profession, the realization is growing that there are no specialists who are able to make any significant contribution in their field of endeavor, unless they are well versed in many fields beyond their own particular specialization. Almost every field has evolved to such a high degree of complexity and difficulty that it takes continuous, unremitting study and learning in many diverse areas to be able to function creatively.

It has variously been estimated that it takes an average of only four to seven years after graduation for the intellectual baggage accumulated during one's educational career to become obsolete, unless the person actively continues his or her education. It is also estimated that in certain technical fields as much as a third of a person's time during the working day has to be devoted to keeping up with the ever-increasing arsenal of new knowledge. And this accumulating information deals exclusively with the area of a person's specialty. For creative thinking, however, one needs competence that spans over a great variety of disciplines. Heedful of this, the creative person makes education and the acquisition of new knowledge a vital part of his or her career. The goal is to become intellectually broad without spreading oneself thin and intellectually deep without becoming pedantic.

The specialist (especially in technological fields) is frequently noncreative because of an inability to see beyond the accepted, narrow areas of his or her particular field of specialization. As William J.J. Gordon, founder of Synectics, Inc., has pointed out, "Many highly trained people naturally tend to think in terms of the dogma of their own technology and it frightens them to twist their conventions out of phase. Their conventions sometimes constitute a background of knowledge upon which they rely for their emotional stability. Such experts do not want cracks to appear. They identify their psychic order with the cosmic order and any cracks are signs of their orderly cosmos breaking up."[9]

Specialists frequently think they know it all and take inordinate pride in personal expertise. When confronted with ideas or approaches that are somewhat unorthodox, they feel compelled to prove, often with convincing logic, that something new "just wouldn't work." Creative persons with a more open mind and global grasp of things often do not accept or believe the arguments that the expert advances. Rather, they move ahead despite the caveats, develop their own methods of approach, and are frequently successful with problems considered insoluble by the experts.

Perhaps the chief danger of specialization is, however, that it emphasizes and demands strict conformity to the accepted and established dogmas and conventions of a field. Learning to comply with the established dogma starts early in the educational career. When it is time to graduate into original production, would-be creative individuals frequently find that they are unable to free themselves from its bondage. Relatively few individuals find the courage to tackle new problems in a new and unconventional manner; only a few transcend their subjugation to the traditional and orthodox and jump ahead into original viewpoints and approaches. It would be beneficial if more people heeded the wise words of the renowned physicist and father of operationalism, P.W. Bridgman, who stated that the most important thing for the creative person to remember is merely "to do his utmost with his mind, no holds barred."[10]

This all is not to gainsay the value of mastering the traditional methods and established canons of a field. Without mastery of the accumulated knowledge of a field—which takes an enormous amount of study and practice—one's compelling hunches may remain mere flashes in the creative horizon. The power of originating ideas without skill and knowledge often prevents their full exploitation. Still, the important point is that one cannot afford to be unduly influenced or enslaved by established knowledge. Creativity is and remains the natural enemy of dogma and conformity.


## CREATIVE MEMORY

The unconscious is a vast storehouse of memories: facts, observations, impressions, ideas, and associations. The creative individual's unconscious is always richly stocked with these, but this does not in itself indicate creative ability. Most of us know people who seem to have all kinds of information and facts at their fingertips, yet have never been able to achieve much in a creative way. The reason for this is that frequently their memory functions as a rigidly ordered storage of deposited concepts, which precludes a flexible and imaginative use of them.

That a prodigious memory can act as a deterrent to creativity has been pointed out by the scientist Ralph Gerard.

> Memory is a desirable attribute; but it is not worthwhile if, as is often the case, one pays for it by having a nervous system that somehow fixes so easily that it loses pliability and the ability to use facts in reasoning and imaging. The general experience has been that the memory wizards are likely to know everything but are not able to do much with it; they are not creative people. There are, of course, notable exceptions; if you happen to be a memory wizard you may also be creative, but the chances are strongly against it.[11]

What makes memory creative is a state of flux or dynamic mobility in its components. The noncreative memory encapsulates or files its data and impressions neatly into independent groupings, clusterings, and categories, all clearly bounded and demarcated. The creative memory, on the other hand, has permeability in its structural boundaries, so that all sorts of related and unrelated data, impressions, and concepts can be cross-indexed and interassociated. Furthermore, in the unconscious of the creative individual, incessant rearranging, pruning, discarding, relating, recombining, and refining of ideas takes place. Such a permeably structured and dynamically fluid memory is hospitable to the formation of new combinations of ideas.

## ABILITY TO THINK IN IMAGES

Creative people rely heavily on internal visual imagery, or "thought-visions." These are, at times, exceptionally clear and vivid; at other times they can be murky and cloudy and rather tenuously and loosely tied to a tumble of vague and meandering thoughts. But whether clear or murky, imagery frequently contains the kernel of a new, original idea.

It was an image analogy that opened the field of atomic physics. To find an explanation for the atomic structure of elements, Niels Bohr used the image of tiny spheres circling in orbits, and to get some insight into the processes within the atom, he made use of an image picture of a miniature planetary system. Einstein likewise claimed that he rarely thought in words at all. Notions came to him in images and only later did he try to express these in words. And there are a whole host of other noted creative individuals on record who stated that first they try to *feel* or *couch in imagery* what they imagine before naming it or formulating a verbal concept of it.

Language, of course, can and does exert a tremendous influence on the unconscious direction of thinking and on how thoughts are finally formed and articulated. But this influence can often be harmful because of the immediate readiness of language to name and to tag labels and concepts on what is perceived internally. This frequently limits any further development of the incipient ideas.

Most people are impatient with the vagueness and incoherency of ideas during the beginning stages of the creative process. They feel immediately compelled to force them into the familiar mold of already existing frameworks, or into language and concepts that invariably fail to do justice to the singular qualities of the perceived novelty. An attempt to crystallize the initially dim or vague creative idea and the eagerness with which most people attempt to snatch it from the void, so to speak, force a premature closure on the idea, which prevents its full range from finding expression.

The precision forced on images and complex thoughts through premature articulation is also fraught with the danger of actually altering them. The renowned mathematician Jacques Hadamaard states:

> I feel some uneasiness when I see that Locke and similarly John Stuart Mill considered the use of words necessary whenever complex ideas are

implied. I think, on the contrary, and so will a majority of creative people, that the more complicated and difficult a question is, the more we should distrust words, the more we should feel we must control that dangerous ally and its sometimes treacherous precision.[12]

In this connection it might be of interest also to cite the philosopher F.S.C. Northrop's ideas on the subject:

> If one wants to get pure facts he must go not to physicists or to chemists or to engineers, but to impressionistic painters. They give us the pure qualities, just the impressions, not the objects we infer from them. . . . The person in our society today who shows us what is directly observed is the impressionistic painter. He just paints this field of immediacy with the sensuous qualities and says, "Now just stop with those and enjoy them." I believe that one of the greatest sources of creativity is to be found in being pulled back by the modern, Western, impressionistic painters to that which is sensed immediately. Only thus are we broken loose from our older inferred theories and enabled to start over again.[13]

What Northrop means is that one should sense what one perceives before articulating it, before making it conceptual or symbolic, or simply before trying to *understand* it intellectually. In this essentially feeling-sensorial fashion one can make perceptions more original and creative. And if individuals can incorporate observations creatively, then they can also immeasurably increase their capacity to think creatively.

## ABILITY TO TOY WITH IDEAS

There is, frequently, a seemingly light side to creative people's involvement in their work. It is shown in the tendency to become lost in what to an outsider would seem an irresponsible playing with ideas, forms, materials, relationships, concepts, and elements, which can be shaped into all kinds of incongruous and imaginative combinations. Creative people know from experience that this apparently purposeless trying out and toying with possibilities strengthens at the same time as it loosens their imaginative powers. Significant creative ideas often emerge out of such a "letting go" exercise.

Toying and improvising also serve some very concrete and immediate purposes. They often help creative individuals to chance upon creative solutions to recalcitrant problems—problems that had previously defied any direct, frontal attack. But most importantly, playful improvising and the willingness to view a problem from unusual angles help to capture a mood that facilitates the flow of ideas. Then one idea will pull out another, and this in turn another, until an idea is hit upon that suddenly commands full attention because this idea represents something truly novel.

Creative individuals have also learned from past experience that these quasi-serious exercises relax the critical and conservative bent of their consciousness. A lighthearted spirit of play frees them from the habits, conditions, and conventions that impede the novel idea. By putting the judicial censor of their conscious minds to sleep, so to speak, creative people can pass over the established order and set the stage for the premiere of novel ideas and solutions.

## ABILITY TO ANALYZE AND SYNTHESIZE

Creative people are able to analyze and break down a problem into parts and to perceive the relationships that exist between the parts and the whole. Analysis is frequently thought of as being diametrically opposed to creativity, but it is part and parcel of the ability to synthesize, and prolonged searching and analysis almost always precede creative synthesis. The analysis of a problem and synthesis of elements condition one another and thus are complementary aspects of a single process in creative problem solving.

Analysis is necessary because it helps the creative person to break the problem down into manageable elements. To synthesize creatively means to combine or rearrange many elements in a way that results in the formation of a new whole. Thus, the creative person has strong dual abilities to abstract the details and particulars and to synthesize or orchestrate a new configuration.

Several experiments have documented that creative people tend to spend more time in the analytical phases of problem solving than do less creative individuals. Researchers S.I. Blatt and M.I. Stein state the following conclusions from their experiments: "Our more creative individuals spent more time and asked more questions that were oriented to analyzing the problem. Our less creative individuals, on the other hand, spent more time and asked more questions that were oriented to synthesizing the information they had. Our observations suggest that the more creative men were 'feeling out' the problem, attempting to understand it, to become one with it; and, after they understood what they were about, they then integrated what they had learned. Consequently, they spent more time analyzing the problem and less time synthesizing the information they had. Our less creative individuals looked as if they were going to wrench the solution from the problem, to dominate it; they 'went after' the answer even before they knew the structure of the problem.''[14]

## TOLERANCE OF AMBIGUITY

One significant reason for the lack of ability to produce creative ideas among many people is their strong preference for precise and concrete thoughts. As a consequence, they tend to prematurely reject notions and ideas that do not fit into what they already know, or that are too intangible or elusive to permit immediate comprehension and categorization. Any state of mind that is vague, misty, or has a veiled sensing of meanings is felt to be scary, uncomfortable, and sometimes even irresponsible by many people because of their predilection for clarity and effortless understanding. Most people find ambiguity threatening; rather, they prefer the tried-and-tested, premixed recipes for their cognitive food. The clearly defined and the familiar have a powerful hold on most people because the new threatens to disturb the secure comfort of the familiar. As William J.J. Gordon explains; "All problems present themselves to the mind as threats of failure. For someone striving to win in terms of a successful solution, this threat evokes a mass response in which the most immediate superficial solution is clutched frantically as a balm to anxiety. . . . Yet if we are to perceive all the implications and possibilities of the new we must risk at least temporary ambiguity and disorder. Human beings are heir to a legacy of frozen words and ways of perceiving that wrap their world in comfortable familiarity."[15] Thus, the hold of the familiar does not give spontaneous free play to the unguided, imaginative promptings that emerge during the creative process.

Truly creative people are not afraid of disorder or ambiguity. On the contrary, they seem rather attracted to phenomena that are not fully ordered or readily comprehended, and prefer cognitively challenging and complex situations. As a result, they are aware of, and open to, the intricate, confusing, and paradoxical qualities of most situations. There is no fear-motivated desire to shut out, ostrich-fashion, any conflicting or ambiguous elements. Like all human beings, creative people seek integration and order, but they are willing to seek it without shutting out the chaotic or the ambiguous, and they have little fear of the unexpected or the unknown.

In their work creative people are always ready to relax any binding habits or patterns and adhere as little as possible to preconceived plans or stereotyped approaches. They also show pliability by being able to simultaneously consider and weigh different and even conflicting concepts and frames of reference.

The creative person also shows greater plasticity and adaptability while creating, and has a healthy respect for groping and uncertainty while forming and ordering thoughts.

## DISCERNMENT AND SELECTIVITY

The overemphasis among the investigators of creativity on the factor of *fluency* may have overshadowed the importance of another attribute, frequently overlooked entirely in the discussions about the creative process. This is the ability to discern the fundamentals of a problem. This factor of discernment—the sensing of relevance, the intuitive feeling of what is significant—is, in some ways, opposed to fluency, but it is perhaps as crucial an attribute for creativity as is fluency.

Creative persons differ from less creative or the noncreative persons in the quality they show in their selection of elements to attend to when confronting a problem. They are better able to judge which factors must be taken into account and which can be neglected or discarded without risk of error. They are also able to discard irrelevant ideas, however original, that simply do not fit, whereas a merely fluent person can get his or her attention tangled up in a jungle of possibilities. In addition, the creative individual shows selectivity in organizing his or her work as economically as the objectives allow. He or she won't allow any superfluous clutter to ruin the elegance of creative solutions.

In creative problem solving, the individual who shows the highest degree of creativity is not necessarily, as a rule, the one who is ebulliently fluent about a problem or the one who reaches the highest degree of abstraction in analysis. Whether fluent or not, individuals who can grasp the heart of the matter, who think most to the point, and who understand the central core of a problem frequently evidence the highest degree of creativity. In creative thinking it is the *quality* of ideas that counts, not necessarily the *quantity* produced. Quantity can add up to nothing if the central point is missed. What basically counts is the discriminative power to see the relevant and qualitatively significant. Creativity is a matter of penetrating to the essence, of discerning the true crux of the problem, rather than merely exhibiting a wealth of notions and ideas.

Creative individuals are guided by a hunch, or intuitive feeling, that enables them to exercise choice, taste, and discernment. Intuitive feelings enable them to make valid distinctions among the complex interplay of elements. Without these feelings, they not only miss much of significance, but they are apt to get lost in a welter of irrelevancies.

## ABILITY TO TOLERATE ISOLATION

When ready to work, creative persons often need a *physical distance* between themselves and the distractions and interruptions of the environment in order to establish a receptive, leisurely mood. They so arrange circumstances that they can be completely alone, undisturbed, and solely concentrated on the creative task at hand.

Biographies of many women creators reveal that not only were they able to tolerate isolation, but they had an insatiable need for solitude. The writer Lillian Hellman, for example, skipped school as a child so she could be alone with her thoughts, and as an adult she frequently spoke of a relentless, driving desire to be alone. The poet Edna St. Vincent Millay needed long periods of withdrawal from others for contemplation and for renewing her energies. Rachel Carson was already a loner as a child. Another writer, May Sarton, felt that constant interaction with others made her feel dispersed, scattered, and in danger of losing her center. The artist Mary Cassatt and the sculptor Malvina Hoffman preferred isolation in order to concentrate without interruption. Even the great psychoanalysts Karen Horney and Florida Scott-Maxwell had to make an extra effort not to withdraw from friends and associates.

In addition to the ability to comfortably tolerate extended periods of physical withdrawal from others, the creative person is also able to tolerate a measure of psychological isolation. If he or she works in an organization, his or her capacity to create also requires *psychological distance* from others. This means that he or she attempts to purge creative deliberations of such considerations as scheduling, costs, a superior's pet ideas about approaches to a problem, and most other prosaic demands of organizational existence. Any extraneous considerations that get grafted onto a problem can block the emergence of novel ideas, by inducing anxiety and guilt feelings in the person for not doing what is expected or demanded. Ideally, creative people should be allowed to let their minds work at an autonomous pace in conformity to their own natural and congenial way. Although creative individuals may be frequently labeled as "lone wolves" because of their required periods of privacy, they are seldom withdrawin, isolated, or uncommunicative.

It should be pointed out, however, that excessively prolonged periods of isolation from others tend to deflate and devitalize rather than enhance the capacity to create. Imagination, when isolated or encapsulated, shrinks and shrivels. It has to be nourished occasionally by active immersion and participation with others. But creative persons cannot allow undue influence from others. They have to retain a safe margin of a social distance in order to do justice to their creative potential.

Since the creative process is in actuality a private and internally motivated affair, creative individuals have to muster the courage and inward strength to face a sense of inner loneliness when venturing into the unknown. Once committed to a one-way road toward the unknown, it is well-nigh impossible for them to fall back on somebody else or to share the responsibility and the development of an idea. Although teamwork projects are so popular these days, creative persons seldom reach their potential through collaboration. In the realm of genuine creativity there is only one solo instrument: the private individual mind and personality of the creative individual. As Carl R. Rogers has stated: "One cannot be creative without being out there and alone; the extent of the aloneness depends on the extent of the creativity. The more creative the act, the more completely alone

one is."[16] And creative people frequently need all the courage and self-confidence they can muster to stand up to the criticisms leveled toward their ideas, for any radically new idea almost always encounters a mountain of resistance and criticism.

The need for isolation and detachment does not mean that creative people can totally dispense with encouragement and recognition. Many things of permanent value have been created only because they received, at one time or another, a great deal of encouragement and stimulation from someone. Yet, in the final analysis, they must rely wholly on themselves. Support and encouragement can be easily withdrawn and can offer only slippery crutches on the fragile terrain of creativity. The condition of self-sufficiency and self-responsibility has to be rooted within the creative person's own being.

## INCUBATION

There comes a time during the creative process when thinking gets ponderous and clogged and when errors start to pile up and no additional new insights occur. This is the time when creative persons cease work on the problem and turn to something more free and different. Many find a welcome change of pace in music, painting, sightseeing, manual tasks, daydreaming, reverie, and so forth. These activities not only provide a refreshing interlude, but enable their unconscious mental activities to operate freely, unrestrained from conscious concentration.

Although creative persons spend a great deal of conscious effort in solving a problem, they realize the limitations of this effort and finally resort to incubation. As the psychologist John M. Schlien points out, "Although he has confidence in his ability, the creative person also has an attitude of respect for the problem and admits the limits of his conscious power in forcing the problem to solution. At some point, called 'incubation' by many who have reported the process, he treats the problem 'as if it had a life of its own,' which will, in its time and in its relation to his subliminal or autonomous thought processes, come to solution. He will consciously work on the problem, but there comes a point when he will 'sleep on it.'"[17]

The unconscious, autonomous thought processes during the incubation period take over and continue solving the problem. When the conscious effort of forcing oneself to solve a problem fails, the incubatory process frequently succeeds.

## ANTICIPATION OF PRODUCTIVE PERIODS

Creative people develop a *retrospective awareness* of periods when problems were solved creatively. The reader might try these suggestions to determine his or her own most productive periods.

- Take note of the methods that have already been successful and those that have failed.
- Try to learn "why" by retracing the routes followed as far back as possible, noting those that were avoided. (Knowledge of one's particular idiosyncrasies and style of creating facilitates the creative process.)
- Schedule creative thinking periods for those times when you have the most favorable mental set for producing ideas.
- Be aware of personal rhythms, peaks, and valleys of output.
- Keep a record of those periods during the day or night when you are most creative. (Then you can establish a pattern and can plan ahead, reserving peak periods for concentration and uninhibited thinking and less-productive time for reading and for gathering information.) Even if you have not kept a timesheet of productive periods, develop a sensitivity to those moods that promise real creative returns, and learn to know when they are approaching.

## OTHER CHARACTERISTICS

Here are some other characteristics that distinguish the more creative individual from the less creative:

- More observant and perceptive, puts a high value on independent "truth-to-oneself" perception. Perceives things the way other people do, but also the way others do not.

- More independent in judgments; self-directive behavior determined by own set of values and ethical standards.

- Balks at group standards, conformity pressures, and external controls. Asserts independence without being hostile or aggressive and speaks mind without being domineering. If need be, is flexible enough to simulate the prevailing norms of cultural and organizational behavior.

• Dislikes to police oneself as well as others and does not like to be bossed around. Can readily entertain impulses and ideas that are commonly considered taboo or that break with convention. Has a spirit of adventure.

• Highly individualistic and nonconventional in a constructive manner. The psychologist Donald W. MacKinnon puts it this way: "Although independent in thought and action, the creative person does not make a show of his independence; he does not do the off-beat thing narcissistically, that is, to call attention to himself. . . . He is not a deliberate nonconformist but a genuinely independent and autonomous person."[18]

• Has wide interest and multiple potential, sufficient to succeed in several careers.

• Constitutionally more energetic and vigorous and, when creatively engaged, can marshal an exceptional fund of psychic and physical energy.

• Less anxious; possesses greater stability.

• Has complex personality: primitive, yet cultured; destructive, yet constructive; deranged, yet sane. Has greater appreciation and acceptance of the nonrational elements in oneself and others.

• Willing to entertain and express personal impulses, pays more attention to "inner voices." Likes to see oneself as being different from others, and has greater self-acceptance.

• Has strong aesthetic drive and sensitivity, and a greater interest in the artistic and aesthetic fields. Prefers to order the forms of own experience aesthetically, and the solutions arrived at must not only be creative, but elegant. Truth has to be clothed in beauty to make it attractive.

• Searches for philosophical meanings and theoretical constructs and tends to prefer working with ideas, in contradistinction to the less creative individual who prefers to deal with the practical and concrete.

• Has a greater need for variety, and is almost insatiable for intellectual ordering and comprehension.

• Possesses a unique sense of humor, and places great value on humor of the philosophical sort.

• Regards authority as arbitrary, contingent on continued and demonstrable superiority. Separates source from content when evaluating communications; judges and reaches conclusions on the basis of the information itself, not on whether the source was an "authority" or an "expert."

# REFERENCES

[1] J.P. Guilford, *Way Beyond the IQ.* (Buffalo, N.Y.: Creative Education Foundation, Inc., 1977), pp. 192.

[2] Leif Fearn, "Individual Development: A Process Model in Creativity," *Journal of Creative Behavior,* 10 (1976), 57.

[3] James H. Austin, *Chase, Chance & Creativity.* (New York: Columbia University Press, 1978), p. 105.

[4] Eugene Raudsepp, "What Makes an Engineer Creative?" *Chemical Engineering,* January 5, 1976, p. 149.

[5] Abraham H. Maslow, *The Farther Reaches of Human Nature.* (New York: The Viking Press, 1971), p. 90.

[6] James H. Austin, *Chase,* p. 64.

[7] L. Goodrich, *Albert P. Ryder.* (New York: Braziller & Company, 1959), p. 22.

[8] Eugene Raudsepp, "What Makes," p. 150.

[9] William J.J. Gordon, *Synectics.* (New York: Harper & Row Publishers, Inc., 1961), p. 96.

[10] P.W. Bridgman, *Reflections of a Physicist.* (New York: Philosophical Library, 1950), p. 56.

[11] Eugene Raudsepp, "What Makes," p. 152.

[12] Jacques Hadamaard, *An Essay on the Psychology of Invention in the Mathematical Field.* (Princeton, N.J.: Princeton University Press, 1945), p. 96.

[13] The Nature of Creative Thinking (monograph), Industrial Research Institute, Inc. (New York: The New York University Press, n.d.), p. 17.

[14] S.I. Blatt and M.I. Stein, "Efficiency and Problem-Solving," *Journal of Psychology*, 48 (1959), 209.

[15] William J.J. Gordon, *Synectics,* p. 36.

[16] Carl R. Rogers, *On Becoming a Person.* (Boston, Mass.: Houghton Mifflin Company, 1961), p. 356.

[17] Eugene Raudsepp, "What Makes," p. 150.

[18] Donald W. MacKinnon, *In Search of Human Effectiveness.* (Buffalo: The Creative Education Foundation Inc., 1978), p. 184.

# 3

# COPING WITH BARRIERS
# TO CREATIVITY

Deficiencies in creative problem solving do not necessarily indicate the absence of creative potential. In most cases they are the result of the many blocks and barriers that tend to inhibit, stifle, distort, and discourage effective creative thinking.

Luckily, once the barriers have been recognized and identified, and a conscious effort is made to remove them, the immediate upsurge of creative output can be considerable.

In a sense, the problem can be likened to a gutter under the eaves of a roof, clogged with dead leaves, twigs, bugs, and sediment. In order for the rainwater to flow through, the gutter must first be cleared. In a similar way, free-flowing creativity and receptivity to new ideas also require the elimination of personal and environmental "sediments."

Although gaining insight into most blocks is sufficient to make better and more productive use of one's latent creative talents, there are some personal blocks that are not only difficult to recognize in oneself, but are difficult to admit and to overcome, even in one's own best interests. Facing them in a conscious, open way, however, and regarding them as problems and challenges to solve, moves one toward a more creative lifestyle.


## PERSONAL BLOCKS


### Faulty Attitude Toward Problems

Life is full of problems and difficulties. Considering the ideal life to be a nirvana-like state in which problems are absent or nonexistent is illusory. We are not vegetables or inanimate objects. Because we can think, feel, respond, remember, plan and because we are social beings intimately involved with others in the enterprise of living, a life without problems, difficulties, and striving against odds would offer no sustenance to our inherent humanness and our creative potentials. For a healthy, fully functioning human being, problems, snags, difficulties, and barriers form an integral and essential part of living. They are there to serve as *challenges* to test and develop our creative capacities. Healthy, creative individuals welcome challenges and feed upon problems; they actively seek them out for the gratifying experience of gaining mastery over them.

Most noncreative people have one cardinal trait in common: they are passive and reactive. They *react* to situations and events, rather than creatively *act* to bring about new circumstances and situations. They expect trouble-free existence to descend upon them through the fiat of some lucky break. Since this kind of living always eludes them, they tend to blame external circumstances or other people for their unhappiness. They cannot see or admit that the real cause of their anguish lies basically in themselves. Even if external circumstances are difficult, their *chronic unwillingness to do something effective about their situation* allows their unrelieved unhappiness to persist. Only when they decide to break out of their self-negating rut and begin to tackle problems actively and creatively can they begin to lay a firm foundation for their psychological health and happiness.

People cannot become strong and healthy by always protecting themselves from unpleasantnesses, failures, disappointments, and hurts. Just as in preventative medicine, poison injected into a living body makes the body resistant to it, so in life, the creative acceptance of the inevitable "poisons of life" makes a person less vulnerable to disappointments and failures and makes them more resistant to misfortune.

Most creative people possess a certain adventurousness of spirit, a genuine willingness to take chances. By adopting this attitude of courage, they almost automatically open and free their imaginations and conquer their fears. The essence of creative growth and zestful living lies in the willingness to occasionally leap into the unknown, in the willingness to give up temporarily the rigid routine of one's living and the solidified habit-patterns that make the future seemingly secure and predictable. Although life is full of risks, it is also full of promises. To partake of the latter, however, one has to be willing to stick one's neck out and take some risks. Balance or wholeness in life is not achieved by shrinking away from bad experiences to preserve the mold into which one's life is cast; it is, rather, achieved by increasing the variety and range of inner and outer living, by immersing oneself unhesitatingly into fresh, new experiences, into experiences that *italicize* the livingness in life. As has been well put: "The only self worth having is one that is interested in many things beyond itself."

## Lack of Self-Confidence

It is seldom recognized how much self-confidence and ego-strength a person requires to do justice to his or her inherent creative potential. Indeed, one of the most serious blocks that inhibits and sometimes even nips a blossoming career of a novice creative person in the bud, is the lack of self-confidence. This lack is often manifested by fear of criticism, fear of others' negative opinions or disapproval, doubt about one's abilities, seeing oneself unfavorably in comparison with others' accomplishments, fear of appearing foolish or unusual, fear of failing to sustain a commitment to action in the face of possible adverse circumstances, and fear of making a mistake.

Rare indeed is the established creative person (and even rarer a beginner) who can consistently maintain a complete detachment from criticism or discouragement. Yet this daringness to transcend accepted or approved patterns of thinking, to call one's own shots, and to stick to one's convictions in the face of possible discouragement or censure, is very necessary in creative work.

Self-confidence is an extremely important personality attribute for creative work, and it can best be developed through experience and exercise. It has been said that nothing breeds success like success; this is probably true. But the corollary—that failure breeds failure—need not be true. If, through continued and persistent application, failures are corrected, high levels of self-confidence and optimism can be achieved. Good creative judgment comes only from experience. And experience comes from poor creative judgment. One should realize that creative progress is made through failures and poor judgments, as well as through successes and good judgments.

Self-confidence cannot be built up entirely alone. A young person especially needs a healthy dose of encouragement and ego-boosting recognition to develop a quiet confidence that he or she will eventually succeed, no matter how many times failures initially occur. Hopefully, in time, most creative people attain a solid confidence in their ideas, work, and capabilities. Once they have attained this confidence, there no longer exists a serious threat to self; situations are perceived and weighed realistically; and there is a ready willingness to risk failure and give free reign to the powers of imagination.

## Fear of Criticism

Because creativity is, in a sense, destructive to the established and accepted, and because there is a natural human tendency to maintain the status quo, the more unique and original an idea is, the more vulnerable it becomes to destructive criticism, disapproval, ridicule, or censorship.

People are, by and large, extremely sensitive to any overt or implied criticism of their ideas. One seldom encounters individuals who have a completely unemotional and objective attitude toward their ideas and who can benefit from criticism that is justified and helpful and ignore the rest. However tough a person may outwardly appear, overcritical attitudes, expressions of cynicism, ridicule, or just plain indifference do have an inhibiting effect. Many original ideas have been repressed through fear of ridicule, and, in extreme cases, cumulative reactions to rebuff or destructive criticism have produced a "drought"—a period in which no new ideas emerge even in the privacy of the individual's own mind.

It is essential that the aspiring creative person learn to evaluate criticism both for content and intent, keeping in mind the fact that people are subject to a variety of inner and outer pressures that make them behave irrationally and destructively. With this degree of objectivity achieved and with the realization that often one's idea is *not* the target of criticism, it is possible to utilize constructive offerings and discard the petty or misplaced.

## Anxiety About Self-Esteem

Another reaction that relates to the fear of criticism has to do with the threat criticism poses to one's self-esteem. Most people are prone to the common fear of being put to shame, or humiliated, or of "making fools of themselves." Situations in which new ideas are expressed engender anxiety through the fear of being considered unintelligent or illogical, fear that the idea is not really "great shakes" after all, and fear of being unable to communicate the idea clearly and persuasively. Recognizing that these anxieties are likely to occur and putting them in their proper perspective can help reduce their damaging effect on creative effort.

## Mistaken Notions About Success

Many people in our society show an inordinate capacity for setting up false expectations, self-defeating goals, and illusory objectives— all based on faulty notions about what, in truly human terms, constitutes success. One of these faulty expectations is that once you gain wealth, power, and fame, you've got it made. Ask almost anyone you know to describe what success means to him or her, and the chances are that the majority of responses would fall into the category of material acquisitions. When William James observed around the turn of the century that "the exclusive worship of the bitch-goddess Success is our national disease," he was referring to the still prevalent idolatry of material success and fame.

Yet the fact is that a great many rich people who have made it in material terms, rarely, if ever, attribute their well-being to wealth. And there are, of course, many wealthy people who, in spite of all the accoutrements of outward riches and success, look as miserable as if they hadn't a thing in the world. They always scramble after more and are chronically dissatisfied with what they have. Their lives point to one of the most pernicious aspects of material possessions: an ever increasing and unquenchable thirst for more and more.

There are many other unfortunate aspects to the single-minded pursuit of material success. Scrambling after material wealth teaches many people to be shrewd, ruthless, crafty, and expedient. They frequently develop an inhuman hardness or insensitiveness toward others and an opportunistic, self-seeking streak that pervades almost everything they do. Then there are those who, in order to achieve material success, are willing to distort and compromise their values and convictions to curry favor with those in positions of wealth and power. By denying their real selves they become the empty husks, the hollow repositories of other people's expectations and demands.

Of late, a healthy development is taking place. An increasing number of people have seriously begun to question the dogma and worship of our popular forms of success, and they openly recognize that their values, interests, and goals diverge radically from the mainstream of our materialistic bent.

In the final analysis, success is a totally personal thing, and each person gives a different definition of the term. The psychologist Lila Swell defines success this way: "A success is any event or experience that you remember as self-fulfilling. It can be a physical, social, intellectual, or aesthetic experience—any event that made you feel successful, good, useful, and/or important."[1] Her definition shows that there are many other dimensions to success than just possessions, fame, status, and popularity.

Creative individuals have a strong and vibrant success-orientation that is directed toward extending the range and quality of those experiences that bring a sense of accomplishment and self-fulfillment. Life requires an endless sequence of new challenges, directions, and goals. Creative people, in fully utilizing their creative and inventive capacities, desire their lives to be a series of continuous self-creations in which they take an active part.

## Tendency to Compare

Creative individuals are true to themselves, true to their inner nature. They seldom have a need to compare abilities or creative achievements with those of others. They are realistically aware of their own capacities as well as their limitations; they are in competition *only* with themselves and with their previous creative accomplishments. There are so many gradations of achievement and success in our complex world that simple and valid comparisons are almost impossible to make.

There is hardly a surer way to diminish the joy of creative attainment than to compare what we have achieved with what some-one else has achieved. Individuals who make a habit of comparing their achievements to those of others and inhibited in their creative undertakings and can never fully savor the accomplishments, no matter how great they are. This is because the act of comparison puts hampers on the mind and makes every success relative. Measuring one's creative performance against the yardstick of someone else's performance can even mean that your brainchild is a relative failure.

## Early Negative Conditioning

Creativity can become easily blocked quite early in life through the unthinking remarks and behavior of adults. The following case histories suggested by the psychiatrist O. Spurgeon English illustrate the negative influence unenlightened parenting can have.[2]

Consider the remarks of a mother of a child of ten who was trying to write stories. When she tried to get her mother to listen the latter said impatiently, "Who would want to read the trash that a ten-year-old would write?" As a result of a few rebuffs such as this the child naturally retired from attempts at writing and never was able to do anything creative later in life even though she had latent interest.

Another example given by English that shows how efforts at doing may be thwarted or how uninspiring adults can be is the story of a youngster who begged his father for a house for his dog. The father bought the materials and the boy looked forward with great anticipation to the day when he and his father would have this building project together. The father, who did not want his nine-year-old son "in the way" while the job was being done, assembled the dog house on the first occasion that his son went to the movies with a friend. He returned home to find the job completed. The son's disappointment was lost on the father, who was so pleased with himself at having completed the construction and who had actually chosen to avoid the patience required for his son's standing by and sharing in some amateurish but valuable efforts in creation. Pity the boy who has never made anything with his hands and received his parents' admiration!

Another clear-cut block to creativity is illustrated in the following history of a young man in his late teens who was beset by doubt, indecision, and feelings of inferiority because his parents had repeatedly asked him, regardless of his undertaking, "Do you think you can do it?" Their distrust of his ability to have a good thought, a useful idea, a constructive endeavor had infiltrated his mind so thoroughly that he was paralyzed and totally unequal to healthy action whether it was mental or physical.

Still another example is that of a woman whose ideas and opinions were belittled during her entire life at home. During the dinner hour, for example, a subject would be under discussion and she would venture an opinion wishing to participate. To this her father would say, "What does a child like you know about it?" or "Of what value, do you think, an adolescent's opinion is to people our age who know about these things?" As might be expected, this woman is today silent and inhibited in expression and opinion at the age of forty-five.

Of such experiences come the blocks, fears, guilts, inhibitions, and projections of old hurts that are truly inimical to creativity.

Not only are these wounded people fearful of criticism, such as they received as children, but any attempts at creative work immediately evoke massive guilt feelings that they may be competing with or even attempting to overthrow a parental figure from his or her position of authority.

## Lack of Self-Knowledge

An increasing number of people these days are asking themselves the all-important questions: "Who am I really?" "Where am I going?" "What should I be doing to lead a creative and zestful life?" "Am I living in a way that is truly satisfying?" As these questions indicate, the primary need for contemporary men and women seems to be to discover the basic requirements of their innermost nature. People these days urgently desire to embark on the road to self-discovery and toward the full exercise and expression of their inherent creative individuality. In short, they want to regain the initiative for life.

The road to self-knowledge and the expression of true individuality is not easy. Heraclitus in the sixth century B.C. observed, "Man is estranged from that with which he is most familiar, and he must continuously seek to rediscover it." Of course, in our times the rediscovery of our real selves is doubly hard because most of us have learned to be more concerned with what we *should* do and be, with what is *expected* of us, than with what our true creative inclinations and needs are. Governed, as most of us are, by "other-direction," by conventions and tradition, we have lost touch with our inner selves.

The psychologist Carl R. Rogers attests that self-knowledge is the basis of psychological health and creative individuality. From the thousands of persons he has treated, he concludes that behind almost every problem there is one central, universal theme: "What is my real self?" "How can I get in touch with this real self, underlying all my surface behavior?" "How can I become myself?"[3]

In Rogers' therapeutic technique, progress is recorded when patients begin to act more like their true selves, dropping the false masks and roles they have hitherto used. Only when they begin to realize how much of their actions have been based on their mistaken notions of what they should be, or of what is expected of them, rather than on what they really are, are they on the road to self-discovery and recovery. As Rogers says, "Often the person discovers that he exists *only* in response to the demands of others, that he seems to have no self of his own, that he is only trying to think, and feel, and behave in a way that others believe he ought to think and feel and behave. Once he has recognized this, half the battle is already won."[4]

According to recent research, individuals who succeed in becoming more aware of their true inner needs are more capable of assuming creative self-responsibility. Psychologist Stella Resnick puts it this way: "Self-responsibility means recognizing that you choose what you do and whom you are. When individuals take responsibility for their lives, they enlarge their alternatives and learn to make choices that enhance and nourish them rather than deplete them. . . . As people pay attention to themselves they begin to recognize how their habitual ways of thinking color their experience, limit their alternatives, and restrict their positive, nourishing, creative ways of being."[5]

Every human being has a true inner self from which his or her creative strength flows. When this inner self is allowed to "pilot the ship," the human venture can be a unique and creative voyage. But this inner self needs to be cultivated, tended to, and brought to full awareness. As the psychologist Magda Proskauer puts it, "Much as a gardener tends to the soil in order that his plants may grow in their own way and season, so attending to the depths of our own nature tills the soil in which, firmly rooted, we can develop into creative individuals."[6]

When individuals tap their central cores—their real inner selves—

they unlock a vast reservoir of their potential, which enables them to fully utilize their creative capacities and take responsibility for their own lives. They have no need to blame other people, their situation, or "fate" when things go wrong; they do not feel as though they are "victims of circumstance." Instead, they can easily marshal inner creative resources to overcome problems and to achieve or ensure their well-being.

## Lack of Positive Feelings and Emotions

In a recent study I conducted with over 1,400 people in almost all walks of life, the following two questions were posed: "What are some of the most pleasant things that have happened to you during your lifetime—things that made you feel exceptionally good about yourself and your life?" and "What are some of the most unpleasant and frustrating things that have ever happened to you during your lifetime—things that made you feel exceptionally bad about yourself and your life?"[7] It came as somewhat of a shock that the "pleasant things" were dispensed with in a few sentences in almost every case, whereas the "unpleasant things" elicited long and elaborate essays. This, in a sense, confirmed my impression that most people are more aware of and more articulate about what bothers, irritates, and frustrates them in their daily transactions, than they are about what they psychologically feed upon.

Creativity requires inner quietude and the accentuation of positive feelings and emotions. One of the fundamental conditions for creativity is receptive concentration. And one cannot achieve this state when bothered by such mental pollutants as worry, resentment, anxiety, loss of self-esteem, and endless internal dialogues with people or situations that have caused distress. We cannot readily entertain new ideas, thoughts, and images when the voices of uneasiness and fear disturb us.

Contradictory as it may seem, many seemingly urgent personal problems and obsessive negative feelings are best solved by putting them aside or temporarily forgetting them. This is the principle of *creative deferment.* When people tend to become obsessed with persistent personal problems, they are less able to see them clearly and act upon them realistically. Frequently, the best strategy is, instead, to substitute some constructive, creative activity in place of brooding over these problems. With the exercise of the free areas of the personality, apparently insurmountable problems get crowded out or shrink to their proper size.

It is a good idea to keep so busy with constructive and creative activities (often in the face of seemingly overwhelming personal problems), that there is no time to examine and reexamine the same old issues. Then, with the gain of self-confidence and self-respect that constructive and productive behavior produces, the original problems (if they are still there) can be solved calmly and systematically. The previously overwhelming and blinding issues will transform themselves into new challenges, which one can then approach with a much more realistic attitude.

## Need for the Familiar

With the passage of time most people tend to become more conservative and habit-prone. We build up comfortable and predictable systems or channels in which our need for stability and security can easily flow and solidify. Some of us even tend to become so "attached" or "devoted" to certain patterns and actions that we are loathe to give them up regardless of their unsuitability in specific situations. If at times something new wells forth, the conflict it creates between the old and secure and the need for new, untried modes of operation often ends with the victory of our conservative impulses, and we continue in the familiar order of things. The inherent danger in this is the possibility that new and worthwhile ideas may be rejected by their originator without trail because they go against established thought or action patterns. Full awareness of this all-too-human tendency is the most effective way to combat it.

## Lack of Disciplined Effort

Absence of consistent and purposive effort can act as a barrier to creative performance. The three common causes are demotivation, self-aggrandizement, and idle fantasy.

Persons are usually demotivated when they have to *force* themselves to do the task at hand, when they lack proper or sufficient stimulation to produce creatively, or when the pictured goal is subjectively seen as not worth the hard work and self-discipline. A clearer sense of personal identity can be obtained through periodic examination of one's personal values, potentialities, temperament, and needs.

A crystallized conception of what one is and wants goes a long way toward promoting greater purposive striving.

Self-aggrandizement usually makes us overestimate the talents, knowledge, and skills we possess. When actual performance does not match our inflated aspirations, we tend to lapse into lassitude or blame others for their obtuseness and lack of appreciation of our "genius." A balanced appraisal of one's assets, as well as limitations, contributes greatly toward self-knowledge and estimation of one's true potentials.

Idle fantasy conjures up the attainment of desired goals without the necessary toil, effort, and discipline that would be required to make them a reality. There are individuals who habitually turn their wishes of accomplishment into fantasy and cannot bring themselves to face the arduous road ahead for actualizing the imagined successes.

### Exesssive Togetherness

Most people in our culture seem to have an all-pervading fear of being alone. Being alone or doing things alone makes them feel that other people regard them as odd, disliked, friendless, or in some way peculiar. The noted Swiss psychiatrist Jurgen Ruesch has perceptively commented on our fear of being alone. "The American becomes uneasy when he finds himself alone. To be left alone is a situation to be carefully avoided; girls accompany each other to the rest rooms or for coffee in the afternoon, the boys and girls have roommates, rarely live alone, and practice double-dating. Not only do bathroom, eating, and social habits of Americans portray this fact, but it can also be observed in the arrangement of houses, or the structure of resort places. In America houses are built close together even if the owners could well afford much larger lots; in public parks and on the beaches picknickers join one another and one group attracts the other, all avoiding isolation."[8]

In our business establishments most employees sit in one big room or if there are partitions, they are made of glass, to have at least visual togetherness, or if they are opaque, they never reach to the ceiling and the usually high noise level assures them that they are not really alone.

The upshot of excessive togetherness and fear of aloneness is that most of us have lost our individuality and our personalities mirror only what goes on in the outside environment, conforming to the dictates of current values and fads in sight, sound, and work. All individual color and creative strength have been drained from us.

We could do no better than to seriously follow the author Mary Ellen Chase's wise advice: "To restore color to our faded personalities and vitality to our languid minds, we must learn to do things, to think things, to become someone, alone. If we are to gain from the world of experience and of people what that world has to offer us, we must frequently withdraw from it."[9] Experience gives us the "negatives" which we can develop into "positives" only through the private "chemistry" of solitary reverie, mediation, and creative daydreaming.

For zestful creative living, privacy needs to be reinstated and cultivated with care. We need to retreat periodically from togetherness, from the tensions, hurry, and stress of collective living and doing, and embark on a return journey into ourselves. In addition to enabling us to regain a valid perspective on our lives, it will provide us with the solitary leisure so necessary for meaningful creative thinking.


## PROBLEM-SOLVING AND ENVIRONMENTAL BARRIERS


### Grabbing the First Idea

Most people, when faced with a problem, tend to grab the first solution that occurs to them and rest content with it. Rare, indeed, is the individual who keeps on trying to find other solutions to his or her problem.

This is especially the case when a person feels under pressure, or when frustrations with a recalcitrant problem are extended over a period of time.

Experience has shown that really effective ideas and solutions come when a quantity of alternatives has been generated. The truly adept creative problem-solver doesn't feel the need to clutch and run with the first notion, but can patiently wait for more unique and effective solutions that occur later in the creative process.

## Premature Judgments

Most individuals have a tendency to jump to conclusions and make premature judgments. Once a judgment is arrived at, they tend to persevere in it even when the evidence is overwhelming that they are wrong. Effective school teachers know the importance of teaching students to refrain from prematurely guessing at an explanation when searching for a principle underlying a situation or event is called for. Because, once they articulate an explanation, they experience difficulty in revising or dropping it in the face of contradictory evidence.

Many interesting psychological experiments have demonstrated the fixating power of premature judgments. In one experiment, color slides of familiar objects, such as a fire hydrant, were projected upon a screen, and people were asked to try to identify the objects while they were still out of focus. Gradually the focus was improved through several stages. The striking finding was this: If individuals incorrectly identified an object while it was far out of focus, frequently they could still not identify it correctly even when it was brought into sufficient focus for easy identification by others who had not prematurely guessed at it. This indicates that considerably more effort and evidence are necessary to overcome an incorrect judgment, hypothesis, or belief than it is to establish a correct one. People who are in the habit of jumping to conclusions frequently close their minds to new information, and limited awareness hampers creative solutions.

## Solution-Mindedness

In his extensive studies on problem solving, the psychologist Norman R. Maier discovered that most individuals, when they are confronted with a problem, feel strong internal pressure to find a solution; in short, they are excessively solution-minded. Once they were encouraged to proceed further and seek a second solution—after they had achieved the first solution—the second solution was invariably a more creative one. Maier concluded that this was because of a shift to problem-orientation: the subjects were no longer driven to find a solution for they had already accomplished that. Now they were relaxed and free to turn the problem over on all sides and entertain different viewpoints. Maier found that this simple shift from solution-mindedness to problem-mindedness increased creative solutions from 16 percent to over 52 percent.[10]

## Over-motivation

There is little doubt that for effective creative performance, some high-octane motivational fuel is necessary. However, some people manage to blunt their effectiveness by either excessive motivation or the desire to succeed too quickly and grandiosely.

Several adverse consequences result from over-motivation. First, over-motivated persons may misunderstand what the real problem is, or they might overlook the obvious, or they may narrow their field of observation too much. They may look for and utilize only those clues that provide a quick solution to their problem, and are thus apt to pass up many things that could lead to a more novel or better solution. The over-motivated person frequently fails to consider a number of possible alternatives in an attempt to pick one, and will therefore latch on to the first one that seems at all workable.

Second, over-motivated persons frequently fail to be global, or generic, in their observations. They fail to see the relationships in the problem components and give inadequate consideration to the basic attributes or ideas that surround the problem. They also fail to make use of the redundancy that coexists with almost all information, and thus become too "literal."

Over-motivation may also result in excessively ambitious goals. Some individuals live in a state of perpetual frustration and disappointment because they want to tackle only very big, very recalcitrant, and very complex projects, pitched unrealistically beyond their capabilities.

## Incessant Effort

Some individuals tend to tackle problems with dogged, incessant effort. Although highly commendable if it enhances one's analytical grasp of a problem, the tendency to keep busy without time out for relaxation and a change of activity frequently can serve as an effective barrier to the emergence of novel solutions to problems.

The person who knows when persistence with a recalcitrant problem begins to bring diminishing returns and who then drops it for awhile, frequently finds that on returning to the problem, a new approach comes with greater ease.

## Concrete or Practical Mindedness

This straight-to-the-point type of barrier insists that instead of roaming imaginatively around a problem, we should immediately get down to facts. It is shortsighted to zero in on an early definition of a problem, because consideration of the broader aspects inherent in almost any problem situation is precluded. "Premature particularization," says William J.J. Gordon, "is very often a symptom of an individual's concern with being impractical."

A.L. Simberg of General Motors has also noted how quick some individuals are to invoke practical and economical judgments when imagination should be given free reign. He illustrates this with the following example: "Our chief engineer gives us the assignment of developing a new product. He tells us that he wants something that is really practical but yet it must be startlingly different. Unfortunately . . . at the sound of the word 'practical,' our imaginations cease to function. Would it not be just as simple to start with the 'startlingly different' idea and engineer this back to practicality? Learn to try to shoot for the single great idea at the outset. Take your chance on the one-in-a-million shot. You can always come back to reality by stages."[11]

In spite of some improvements in the quality of our organizational life styles, people still tend to feel slightly guilty if they enjoy what they're doing, or if they fail to produce as fast as their colleagues do, or if they feel that what they're contributing is not of immediate practical value.

## Intolerance of Complexity

The noted scientist Ralph W. Gerard once said, "The great danger of the intellect is that one can always subdivide the universe in some way, and 'nature does not come as clean as you think.' We can fool ourselves by dividing the universe in particular ways, by the 'Twenty Questions' technique. Most of our thinking is in terms of black or white, up or down, and like dichotomies, with little grading; and such categories put a straight-jacket on our mind which impedes the arrival of the new."[12]

A person who wants to be a creative problem-solver should be able to tolerate a high degree of complexity, to perceive a great variety of possibilities, and be able to consider and balance different or even contradictory frames of reference, concepts, elements, and so forth, without prematurely discarding those that do not permit easy comprehension and categorization. Often, when difficulty is experienced in maintaining an open flow of relationships or multiple possible relationships simultaneously, the tendency is to "run away," that is, to "close out" the problem by accepting a simple or stereotyped solution.

### Habit Transfer

One very common obstacle to creative problem solving is the influence of past conditioning of our thoughts and actions when solving a new problem. When this happens, we attack new problems only with methods and procedures that proved successful before, rather than trying new, untried approaches that might have greater potential for successfully solving the problem at hand.

Individuals with strong analytical ability and ego-involvement with previous successes are prone to have this block. Although they are fully able to reduce the new problem to its fundamentals, they may feel afraid of any new creative synthesis which may not "live up" to their past performances.

One can become more aware of this tendency toward habit transfer by occasionally asking oneself the following questions:

- Did the problem seem so familiar that I automatically accepted a solution based on previously successful approaches, rather than investigating other avenues of approach?
- If I relied solely on a past approach, was it out of a considered decision, or was it to avoid the effort and insecurity that a new approach might entail?
- Has familiarity with an area caused me to seize upon a few basic approaches to the extent that I may fail to recognize situations in which they do not apply?

### Smugnosis

"Smugnosis" is an affliction that adversely affects judgment. It propels individuals to arrive at negative conclusions, based on the omniscient trust they have in their own store of information and knowledge. Individuals with advanced formal education and degrees are particularly susceptible to smugnosis.

Only a few years before the first atomic explosion, an internationally respected scientist and authority of atomic energy publicly declared that a millennium of research and development effort would be required to develop an atomic bomb.

Both the present-day rapid dynamics of change and the spreading disease of smugnosis prompted the writer Elbert Hubbard to come up with the following very apt observation: "The world is moving so fast these days that the man who says it can't be done is generally interrupted by someone doing it."

### Feelings of Dependency

With the increasing complexity of modern society, the network of our mutual dependencies is increasing. Yet these dependencies are frequently the very enemies of creativity.

Let us briefly examine how dependency expectations operate in business and industrial environments. Instead of assuming that people are responsible and in control of their own actions on the job, they assume, and often correctly, that control and responsibility are the work of others who have been assigned the responsibility for specific tasks and projects. There they wait to be directed and stimulated by others in the organizational network in which they see themselves suspended. Rather than being able to evaluate their work based on their own immediate feelings of appropriateness, they tend to rely on the opinions and judgment of others. They are, thereby, encouraged and challenged not to be independently creative persons, but to be passive, dependently adaptive individuals who must use their energy and minds to adjust to groups and individuals who are higher in the organizational pecking order. They feel they must suppress their creative individuality in order to keep in line with the multiple group-belongings necessary for keeping their jobs and supporting their organizational identity.

Dependency is also reinforced through the fear of failure. The degree of individual responsibility for failure is considerably lessened if an idea and its subsequent implementation have been approved and decided upon "in a committee," and if the individual can claim immunity through not having acted independently. The temptation, in the face of failure, to ease one's ego by saying "it was their idea," exists in most of us. By the same token, we often accept and use ideas and methods we know are inferior to our own in order to be able to "share the blame" should things go wrong.

## No Time for Creative Thinking

Most of us who work in organizations are constantly interrupted by telephone calls, urgent memos, visits by colleagues, idle chatter, unscheduled meetings, letter-writing, and a whole host of "administrivia" that leave little time for creative thinking. One effective way of overcoming this is to define and redefine one's primary functions so that time is reserved for creativity, and then sell or negotiate this with one's superior.

Ronald Clark reports that Albert Einstein used to receive enormous amounts of correspondence. This included just plain fan mail and all sorts of requests for Einstein to speak, make appearances, support causes, loan money, and write letters of recommendation. When Einstein was deeply involved in working on the general theory of relativity he needed to work alone and undisturbed much of the time. How to handle this flood of correspondence? Einstein kept a big meat hook hanging from the ceiling above his desk and he would, when he was particularly occupied, simply hang whole packages of unopened letters up on the meat hook for future attention. A visitor, noticing huge bungles on the hook, asked him what he did when the meat hook was full. Einstein answered with a simple, "Burn 'em!"[13]

Whether we can really follow Einstein's example in a corporate set-up is a moot question. What it indicates, however, is that we know we have more leeway than we think we do in choosing the way we respond and react to outside expectations and demands. In addition, setting of priorities and other time-management techniques enable us to reserve solid blocks of uninterrupted time for creative thinking.

## Competition Versus Cooperation

Paradoxically, both competition and cooperation, usually considered to be polar opposites, can equally inhibit creativity. An overemphasis on cooperation frequently means that individuals must inhibit or temper their initiative, resources, and creative ideas in order to fit in or sometimes even to keep their jobs.

Overemphasis on competition usually involves win-lose dynamics. Individuals are made to feel that they are working against each other and that they have to come out on top. With this attitude the quality of solutions to problems, or the excellence of the product to be created, becomes of secondary importance.

Of the two, cooperation or competition, the latter is more crippling to creativity and more ingrained in our organizational value systems. As the psychologist A.R. Wight puts it, "Our society is so imbued with the spirit of competition, and so convinced of its merit, that eliminating the win-at-any-cost competition from an individual's repertoire of values, attitudes, and behavior becomes a major undertaking. The attitude that competition is 'good' is generalized to include all competition, or it is argued that man is by nature competitive, that competition is instinctive. But most human behavior is learned behavior, and competition is taught, valued, and rewarded in our society. . . . It is quite possible that this emphasis on winning is associated with or contributes to the development of desire for power, status, and prestige, which also interfere with creative group performance. These personal objectives take precedence over organizational objectives in any situation, and politics and infighting become the rule."[14]

## Lack of Interest in Problems

Most people who work in organizational or corporate setups spend most of their time working on problems dictated by the needs and requirements of the organization. This often means that they are called upon to tackle problems that do not hold any particular interest for them, with consequent reduction in creative performance. The psychologist Richard N. Wallen explains it this way:

> One serious block occurs when we are pushed to solve a problem that doesn't concern us. When we are fascinated, we feel the problem pulling us. We do not feel pushed into it. The fascinating problem is one that we choose, one that somehow belongs to us. People do not need to be driven to do things that have an intrinsic attraction. . . . I do not believe that people can be pushed into being creative. Faced with a demand for a solution to a problem they have not chosen, people may come up with ideas. But I do not think that they reach their best creative thinking under such conditions.[15]

## Fantasizing Is Worthless

Daydreaming, reverie, and speculative meanderings have always been the forerunners of new creative works. Most creative products were at one time merely the musings and fantasies of an actively receptive, imaginatively far-ranging mind. Our culture, however, discourages daydreaming. It is still widely regarded not only as a waste of time, but as indicative of a lack of maturity, if not serious psychopathology.

In most of our business organizations, individuals who are physically active paper shufflers and who move around, pace the corridors, and visit with their colleagues are considered valuable. On the other hand, the employee who quietly sits and thinks at his or her desk and occasionally stares into space, is considered suspect or lazy. Because of our empty and faulty organizational insistence on giving the outward appearance of looking busy all the time, the person who tries to do some creative thinking, feels uncomfortable and guilty, particularly if the boss happens to survey the scene. This is only one of the many ways in which the business atmosphere discourages creative ideation.

## Busyness

Most of us seem to equate busyness with effectiveness. We feel uneasy or guilty if we are not constantly doing something, busily occupied with myriads of tasks. We seem to feel that every minute of our lives has to be "constructive" in some way. Even in our hobbies, play, and recreation, the dead seriousness about a specific goal or practical accomplishment to be reached frequently mars the pleasure we ought to derive from what essentially should be pure relaxation for recharging the creative batteries.

Although our utilitarian and practical orientation seems so commendable to many people, the renowned critic Walter Kerr has eloquently argued that our unrelenting monomania with what is practical may well account for the decline of true pleasure, the absence of meaningful leisure, and the consequent vague discontent that seems so endemic in the United States today. Because of Kerr's sharpness of perception, he is quoted here at length:

> In a contrary and perhaps rather cruel way, the twentieth century has relieved us of labor without at the same time relieving us of the conviction that only labor is meaningful.

We are all of us compelled to read for profit, party for contacts, lunch for contracts, bowl for unity, drive for mileage, gamble for charity, go out for the evening for the greater glory of the municipality, and stay home for the weekend to rebuild the house.

It is probably that our very awareness of the existence of pleasure that we are either postponing or denying ourselves adds to the tensions induced by unrelieved labor. We feel guilty when we take our pleasure, because there is so much work we might do. We feel guilty when we work so hard, because our lives may depend upon pausing for pleasure. The two guilts are incompatible, and we suffer further from the head of steam their mutual abrasiveness builds up.

Guilt is a strange word to have become associated with the experience of pleasure. It suggests, to begin with, that we have a deep conviction of time wasted, of life wasted, of worthwhile opportunities missed, whenever we indulge ourselves in a mild flirtation with leisure.

What twentieth-century man holds to be important and worthwhile is usefulness, the profit that may be extracted from an experience or a possession.

The contemporary evidence seems to suggest that something other than an occasional crackup threatens us, that we are more widely menaced by a near-universal ennui, an ennui rooted in a contradiction. Even as we hurl ourselves feverishly into more and more work, we are quietly aware of a stirring nausea, of a faintly sickening distaste for the work we must do, the world we must do it in, and the selves we must live with while we are doing it.

The habits that keep us alive are the habits that keep us unhappy.[16]

Just how harmful our preoccupation with "constructive activity" really is, can be illustrated by the very prevalent "retirement neurosis" in our culture. Unaccustomed to creative leisure and playfulness, a great many men and women, when thrown on their own resources upon retirement, suddenly find themselves confronting a painful, debilitating void, an unbearable boredom. It is as if all interest, all meaning had suddenly dropped from under them. This results in feelings of deep depression and often in a rapid deterioration of their psychological as well as their physical health.

Hyperactivity is in reality an empty affair, and it has contributed to our general restlessness and our inability to receptively concentrate on any one thing for any length of time. Erich Fromm has well described how hyperactivity actually amounts to doing nothing. As he says, "We are always busy, but without concentration. When we do one thing, we are already thinking of the next thing, of the moment when we can stop doing what we are doing now. We do, if possible, many things at the same time. We eat breakfast, listen to the radio, and read the newspaper, and perhaps at the same time we carry on a conversation with our wife and children. We do five things at the same time, and we do nothing. Nothing, in the sense that we do it as a manifestation of our real powers, of which we are the masters. If one is truly concentrated, the very thing one is doing at this moment is the most important thing in life. If I talk to someone, if I read something, if I walk—whatever it is, if I do it in a concentrated fashion, there is nothing more important than what I am doing in the here and now."[17]

## Isolation of the Creative Person

Creativity feeds on the stimulation and cross-fertilization of ideas that a congenial group of like-minded individuals can provide. In many organizations, unfortunately, such channels for creativity-stimulating experiences are lacking. This was expressed with lucid directness by one creative specialist in a medium-sized organization. "We have many specialists in our organization. I happen to be one of these. Each of us can understand things from his particular angle; all the others understand things from their particular angles. When I get a bright idea, there is no one to whom I can go and be really understood. What's creative to me is not seen as creative by anyone else because they don't have the background to know what I had to do to get to where I got; they can't see what's new about it. In these circumstances, it's easy to lose interest in creating simply because you can't really share it. There's probably a lot of creativity in our organization we can't ever see because we individually don't know enough to recognize it."[18]

## Fear that Ideas will be Stolen

There are individuals who feel they will only have a few good ideas which they must jealously guard, or they might be stolen. While this can be, on occasion, a realistic fear, there are a multitude of ways to safeguard against it. Affixing one's signature to an idea expressed in writing and then circulating it among several people, is frequently sufficient for protecting ownership.

Creative people behave in a different fashion. They act as if their supply of ideas is endless, and it usually is for them. They don't have to waste time and energy protecting one idea; rather, they use their energies for producing more. Not only can ideas be smothered to death by overprotection, but a suspicious and overcautious attitude may even seriously inhibit one's power to produce them.

### Risky Road of Organizational Channels

A new idea frequently has to travel through layers and layers of supervisors and decision makers before further development is approved on the idea. The real risk this poses to the idea has been pointed out by numerous creative individuals. One of them expressed it as follows:

> Suppose I get an idea I want to explore. It isn't ready to be put into formal shape. I just want to clear it as an idea and to find out whether individuals up the line in the organization would support it. First I talk with my group leader. Let's suppose he and I get along well; our minds and personalities click. He takes the idea to the section head. The group leader and the section head make up a new pair for doing business around this area. I like my group leader because I'm confident he doesn't change into another sort of person when he enters this new situation, but both he and I know there is a long gauntlet ahead where there can be a break in the pairs. From section chief, a new pair is formed with the department supervisor, then between the supervisor and department director, then between the department director and the technical director, and then between the technical director and the division manager. This is just inside our division on the way up—six pairs! The idea might involve still more pairs beyond that and then again more pairs on the way down, if the idea was the kind that would involve other divisions of the company. A break anywhere along the line could be critical. My idea could get distorted all out of shape or lost altogether since it is not worked out in its ramifications and is easily subject to attack. It can become a scapegoat for most anything. Given these circumstances, you can see I'm not going to be spouting ideas very often.[19]

### Other Blocks and Barriers

- Accepting the idea that the problem is too difficult and beyond one's understanding.
- Superficiality—shallowness, incompleteness, and hastiness in thinking and problem solving.
- Judging too quickly.
- Failure to acquire sufficient information to solve a problem.
- Failure to relate the problem to its environment.
- Inability to see the problem from various viewpoints.
- Inflexible use of problem-solving strategies.
- Belief that humor is out of place in problem solving.

- Inability to abandon an unworkable approach.
- Poor language skills to record or express ideas.
- Failure to distinguish between cause and effect.
- Too much faith in statistics.
- Difficulty in seeing remote relationships.
- Failure to use all the senses in observing.
- Belief that it is not wise to doubt or to question.
- Belief that inquisitiveness is impolite.
- Imitation of the behavior patterns of others.
- Fear of asking questions that show ignorance.
- Undue concern with the opinion of others.
- Freezing of behavior into rigid patterns.
- Excessive involvement with others and neglect of own needs.
- Fear of being a pioneer or "first" in a field.
- Excessive desire or preoccupation with security.
- Fear of exploring the unknown.
- Excessive dependence on authorities.
- Negativity toward the new and novel.
- Attitude of "play it safe."
- Lack of initiative or self-starting ability.
- Fear that one's ideas will be stolen.
- Deeply rooted internal prejudices, biases, and superstitions.
- Laziness—general lack of drive, incentives, ambition.
- Lack of self-awareness and self-orientation.
- Lack of spontaneity—inability to let capacities flow of themselves.
- Rigid defenses, inhibitions, and fears.
- Narrow, truncated interests.
- Poor health—physiological and psychological problems—illness, tension, pain, anxiety, and so forth.
- Inability to relax.
- Boredom, passivity, chronic fatigue.
- Inability to distinguish reality from fantasy.
- Lack of appreciation of the value of imagination, fantasy, humor, dreaming, inability to open-mindedly tune in to "messages from within."
- Failure of management to recognize and reward creative ability.
- Autocratic boss who values only his or her own ideas.
- Lack of interest in off-beat ideas.
- Apathy and complacency.
- Lack of long-range objectives.
- General distrust of originality.
- Emphasis on immediate functional utility of ideas.
- Tendency of management to tell the creative persons what to do and how to do it.
- Discouragement of experimentation.

- Frequent changes of key decisions.
- Lack of effective communications between employers and management.
- Reluctance of management to take chances.
- Poor handling or outright misappropriation of credit.
- Tendency to overdevelop routines and standard practices.
- Problems of creative work settled by fiat from above.
- Creativity—within limits.
- Overemphasis on teamwork.
- Management's tendency to look at a proposal with one question in mind, "What's wrong with it?"
- Management's attitudes: "It was good enough ten years ago, it's good enough now," or "We are not going to take any chances."
- Inflexible work schedules.
- Stagnation.
- Lack of cooperation and trust among colleagues.
- Inflexible organizational structure.
- Competition with "promoter-type" colleagues.
- Insistence upon immediate results.
- Resistance to change.
- Poor attitudes of management toward creative people.
- Lack of appreciation and recognition by management of creative contributions.
- Lack of creative challenge and encouragement.
- Poor handling of credit.
- Loss of identification with contributions.
- An attitude of ignoring individuals.
- Fear of the speculative.
- Preoccupation with the ability to get along with others.
- Too much steering by supervisors.
- Tight project management.
- Nonrecognition in any manner of the extra effort required.
- Isolation of the creative specialist.
- Absence of creative catalysts.
- Feeling of having to work within the prejudices and preconceptions of management.
- Lack of understanding of the really creative person and his or her motivation.
- Lack of support for long-range, basic planning.
- Reason, logic, numbers, utility, practicality are good; feeling, intuition, qualitative judgments, pleasure are bad.
- Mistaken notions regarding talent.
- Lack of tolerance for and interest in diverging views.
- Need for the familiar—habit-proneness.
- Need for excessive order.

- Incessant effort—compulsivity.
- Fear of supervisors.
- Distrust of colleagues.
- Jealousy of colleagues.
- Apathy and complacency.
- Fear of "wasting time" on the part of supervisors.
- Inflexible or inadequate use of intellectual problem-solving strategies.
- Lack of questioning attitude.
- Overspecialization.
- Too many "hack" assignments.
- No special awards for creative achievement.
- Too many inaccurate schedules.
- Lack of authority to match responsibility.
- Too many deadline crises.
- Lack of participation in the selection of projects.
- Absence of a quiet area for concentration, free from noise and motional type of distractions.

# REFERENCES

[1] **Lila Swell,** *Success: You Can Make It Happen.* New York: Simon & Schuster, 1976, p. 46.

[2] **O. Spurgeon English,** from a talk delivered at Princeton University, Princeton, N.J., March 16, 1965.

[3] **Carl R. Rogers,** *On Becoming a Person.* (Boston: Houghton Mifflin Company, 1970), p. 108.

[4] Ibid., p. 110.

[5] **Eugene Raudsepp,** *The Essential Self.* (to be published) (Los Angeles, California: Price/Stern/Sloan Publishers, Inc.).

[6] **Herbert A. Otto** and **John Mann,** eds., *Ways of Growth.* (New York: Pocket Books, 1971), p. 34.

[7] **Eugene Raudsepp,** "A New Look at Human Values," (unpublished paper), Princeton, N.J.: Princeton Creative Research, Inc., February 1980.

[8] **Jurgen Ruesch,** *Communication.* (New York: W.W. Norton & Co., Inc., 1951), p. 110.

[9] **Eugene Raudsepp,** "Daydreaming: Wasted Time or Your First Step toward Success?" *Success Unlimited,* November 1975, p. 67.

[10] **Norman R. Maier,** *Problem Solving and Creativity in Individuals and Groups.* (New York: Brooks/Cole Publishing Co., 1970), p. 189.

[11] A.L. Simberg, "Obstacles to Creative Thinking," in Gary A. Davis and Joseph A. Scott, eds., *Training Creative Thinking.* (New York: Holt, Rinehart & Winston, 1971), pp. 119–135.

[12] Sidney J. Parnes and Harold F. Harding, eds., *A Source Book for Creative Thinking.* (New York: Charles Scribner's Sons, 1962), p. 120.

[13] Ronald Clark, *Einstein, The Life and Times.* (New York: World Publishing Co., 1971), p. 68.

[14] A.R. Wight, "What Does Industry Want—Creativity?" (unpublished paper), pp. 16, 21.

[15] Richard N. Wallen, "Unlocking Human Creativity," *Machine Design,* March 20, 1958, p. 136.

[16] Walter Kerr, *The Decline of Pleasure.* (New York: Simon & Schuster, 1962), pp. 34–42.

[17] Harold H. Anderson, ed., *Creativity and Its Cultivation.* (New York: Harper & Brothers, 1959), p. 49.

[18] Ross L. Mooney, "On Meeting Cultural Blocks to Creativity" (unpublished paper), n.d., p. 6.

[19] Ibid., p. 9.

# 4

# STIMULATING CREATIVITY

A great many idea-finding strategies, tactics, and procedures have been devised to generate creative solutions to problems. They have been, and can be, used with simple problem-solving tasks as well as with difficult creative challenges. The basic benefits of these various techniques are that they

- promote increased effectiveness in problem solving.
- provide help when ideas are not forthcoming, or when the creative process appears to be bogged down.
- produce a multiplicity of ideas and problem solutions—solutions which might not otherwise occur in the course of the person's usual problem-solving approach.
- encourage the finding of unusual, nonobvious, and nonhabitual approaches and combinations of ideas; they help overcome rigidity and habitual mind-sets.
- help a person to break through the implied boundaries of a problem.
- help a person *not* to overlook possible new approaches, concepts, or viewpoints for problem solution.
- encourage mental gymnastics and stimulate imagination.

Some of the more fruitful strategies and self-prodding techniques to trigger new ideas are described in this chapter. They can be used separately or in various combinations to trigger creative conceptualization.

The techniques and strategies are only means to an end, not the end itself. They should be considered as a supplement and not a substitute for intuitive or inspirational idea finding, and their basic aim is to help you to increase the openness and receptivity of your mind.


## BRAINSTORMING

One of the best and most widely used idea-stimulating techniques is *brainstorming,* developed by Alex F. Osborn in 1939.[1] It can be used either by groups or individuals, and the rules are few and simple.

1. Quantity not quality, of ideas is the goal. The greater the number of ideas, the more likelihood of arriving at really original and effective ideas. It is far easier to pick a prizewinner from a long list of alternative ideas than it is to arrive at one when the number of ideas is small.

2. No judgment or evaluation may take place until all the ideas are in. This is the most crucial rule of brainstorming because most people habitually evaluate ideas while in the process of thinking them up. Failure to suspend criticism is, according to Osborn, "like trying to get hot and cold water from one faucet at the same time: the ideas are not hot enough; the criticism is not cold enough; so your results are tepid!"

3. Unusual or fanciful ideas are encouraged. As a matter of fact, the wilder the ideas the better. Experience has shown that seemingly unfeasible, off-beat ideas have frequently been adopted as the best of the lot, or they may trigger in others additional ideas which might not otherwise have been thought of. For example, in one brainstorming session the following problem was posed to the participants:

"If 700 miles of outside telephone wires were coated with three inches of frost so that long-distance calls could not be made, how would you restore normal service as fast as possible?"

In fifteen minutes, over twenty possible solutions were given. Among them were

    a. Charge the wire with a heat-building current that would melt the frost off.

    b. Put smudge pots or fires on ground beneath wires.

    c. Use flame throwers or blowtorches.

    d. Have crews knock off with long poles.

    e. Use infrared heat units to defrost wires.

    f. Have a helicopter fly over so that its downdraft would melt the ice.

This last idea met with laughter. And yet, when that same problem actually developed in the Northwest a few months later, the helicopter solution actually turned out to be the best solution.

4. Where a group is involved, members are encouraged to "piggy-back" on others' ideas, adding features or variations. "Hitchhiking" on one another's ideas can add invaluable combinations or improvements and this rule is one of the most valuable features of brainstorming.

## THE REQUIREMENTS
## OF SUCCESSFUL BRAINSTORMING

Much of the success of a brainstorming session depends on the choice of a group leader. He or she can make or break a session. Some of the attributes the group leader should possess are: (1) the ability to handle monopolizers and evaluators as well as to bring out the more taciturn and reserved participants; (2) the ability to retain enthusiasm and energy throughout the session; (3) the ability to quickly recognize the potential in ideas offered and have ideas of his or her own to articulate, should the flow of ideas slow down; (4) the skill of encouraging free-wheeling ideation while at the same time keeping the discussion from becoming a long-winded discourse by one or more members; (5) the capacity to maintain a *positive* stance toward all ideas offered; (6) the absence of the need to dominate or hog the center stage; (7) a friendly, sharp-witted attitude that stimulates the lethargic, negative, or indifferent participants and tranquilizes the overebullient monopolizers; and (8) the ability to balance the far-fetched or ridiculous ideas with those that show common sense. At times when the apparently ridiculous contributions seem to gain the upper hand, the group leader should attempt to demonstrate the practical potential of some of these ideas by modifying them accordingly or toning them down to reality.

A secretary should be chosen who can record the ideas suggested in full view of the participants. The ideas should be numbered for later combinations or clusterings. Ideas often come at such a rapid rate that they are missed or not heard by some participants—hence the recommendation of recording them in full view.

The group size for a brainstorming session is a variable factor. Although the most workable number of participants is between seven and twelve people, successful sessions have been conducted with a smaller or a much larger number of participants. The important thing is that there should be a steady flow of ideas, so the group size should be determined by the expected fluency of ideas of the participants being invited. The simplicity or complexity of the problem is also a determining factor. The more complex or technical the problem, the larger, ideally, should be the participating group.

A group of individuals with mixed backgrounds and experience is generally good for more general problems, whereas more specific and complex problems are best tackled by people who have a more specialized understanding of the problem.

Participants should be of approximately equal status. The presence of one or two bosses or superiors can have an inhibiting effect. As one expert on brainstorming put it: "If there is one piece of brass in a twelve-man brainstorming session, there will be eleven brass polishers!"

The brainstorming technique is most effective with a general, simply stated problem, or a well-defined and clearly stated portion of a more complex problem. Any background explanation about the problem should be done in advance of the session. When ready to start the idea-generation phase, the problem statement should be brief and straightforward. Too detailed an explanation immediately before ideation tends to lock participants into a judicial mode that is inhibitive of idea fluency. Some effective ways of phrasing a problem are: "How else could we? . . ." "How would you improve upon? . . ." "In what other ways can we? . . ."

## SOME PITFALLS TO AVOID

- Failure to get management backing for a brainstorming program.

- Failure to train participants adequately in brainstorming principles.

- Failure to orient the problem properly, or to make it specific enough.

- Overselling the benefits of brainstorming, which builds up unrealistic expectations.

- Too short a time devoted to the brainstorming session. Experience has shown that only when the top-of-the-head ideas from memory are exhausted is the stage set for combining, adapting, and rearranging thoughts and ideas—the essential building blocks of new ideas.

- Failure to emphasize that not all ideas offered have to be original. What is obvious to one person may be not so commonplace to another. Sometimes with a minor modification, a commonplace idea turns into an original and workable idea. Improvements on, or combinations of, ideas already offered have frequently more value than do the original ones. Strictly taboo are statements such as: "That's the same as. . . ." or "What's the difference between that and? . . ." or "That's already been covered. . . ." and so forth.

- Failure to evaluate ideas creatively.

- Submitting a list of ideas to management without careful evaluation and screening.

- Lack of follow-up in the development and implementation phases of ideas.

- Failure to report to participants what action is being taken on ideas.

## ALEX F. OSBORN'S CHECKLIST
## FOR NEW IDEAS

Alex F. Osborn has developed a general checklist that is applicable to a great variety of problems. Although its main purpose is to trigger ideas for the improvement of objects or processes, with a little imagination it can be adapted to yield solutions to problems in social, educational, and personal areas as well.[2]

- *Adapt?* Put to other uses? New ways to use as is? Other uses if modified? What else is like this? What other idea does this suggest? Does past offer parallel? What could I copy? Whom could I emulate?
- *Modify?* New twist? Change meaning, color, motion, sound, odor, form, shape? Other changes?
- *Magnify?* What to add? More time? Greater frequency? Stronger? Higher? Longer? Thicker? Extra value? Plus ingredient? Duplicate? Multiply? Exaggerate?
- *Minify?* What to subtract? Smaller? Condensed? Miniature? Lower? Shorter? Lighter? Omit? Streamline? Split up? Understate?
- *Substitute?* Who else instead? What else instead? Other ingredient? Other material? Other process? Other power? Other place? Other approach? Other tone of voice?
- *Rearrange?* Interchange components? Other pattern? Other layout? Other sequence? Transpose cause and effect? Change pace? Change schedule?
- *Reverse?* Transpose positive and negative? How about opposites? Turn it backward? Turn it upside down? Reverse roles? Change shoes? Turn tables? Turn other cheek?
- *Combine?* How about a blend, an alloy, an assortment, an ensemble? Combine units? Combine purposes? Combine appeals? Combine ideas?

## ATTRIBUTE LISTING

In this technique, developed by Robert Crawford of the University of Nebraska, the major attributes or characteristics of a product, object, or idea are isolated and carefully listed. The next step involves the consideration and modification of each of these characteristics. After this exercise all of those combinations are evaluated according to the limitations posed by the problem situation.[3]

As an example, consider the attributes of the screwdriver a few decades ago: (1) round steel shank, (2) riveted wooden handle, (3) flattened wedge-shaped end, (4) powered manually, and (5) torque developed by twisting action. All of these attributes have been changed and the result has been a much more efficient product. In place of the round shank there is now a hexagonal cross section that can be easily gripped with a wrench and additional torque supplied. The wooden handle has been replaced by a safer, lighter, and more durable molded plastic. Instead of the flattened wedged-shaped end, we now have the Phillips head, clutch head, hex head, etc. Electric motors with torque-limited clutches provide the power for industrial screw drivers. "Yankee" type screw drivers develop torque by pushing rather than by twisting.

A simple experiment has demonstrated that thinking in terms of attributes rather than in terms of labels is infinitely superior for creative ideation.[4]

One group was asked to name all possible uses for paper. The other group was asked to list all possible uses for something called "Material X," for which was given a list of certain qualities and attributes. "Material X" was, of course, paper. The second group, because its thinking was not circumscribed by the label "paper," was able to produce many more uses for the material than did the first group.

There are countless examples of what has been accomplished with paper. Paper has been made into railroad car wheels with a life-expectancy of several thousand miles. It has served as the major structural material in churches, as well as in factory chimneys. It has been used as a paving or surfacing material, and a watchmaker in Dresden, Germany, has used paper to make several watch parts. Paper horse shoes were once quite common in Europe. There are probably thousands more practical uses for paper in its various forms that have thus far not been imagined.

## MORPHOLOGICAL ANALYSIS

This technique, developed by Fritz Zwicky at the California Institute of Technology, consists of two steps: defining the problem in terms of its parameters or dimensions, and then visualizing all possible combinations of the parameters by aid of a matrix.

In a problem that has only two parameters, the matrix is drawn in a form of a large square divided into a series of smaller squares.

Kenneth L. Pittman of Creative Synergetic Associates illustrates this technique by the process of choosing the proper paneling for a basement.[5] The two main characteristics of the paneling are: (1) surface appearance, and (2) color of stain. The matrix, then, would be represented as shown in Table 1.

As can readily be seen from Table 1, there are a total of sixteen possible combinations one can choose from. By introducing a third variable, for example, material (see Table 2), the possible combinations are increased to sixty-four. To manipulate the three-variable matrix with ease, Pittman suggests that they be listed on separate sheets of paper. Then, by holding one sheet fixed, and moving the others up or down, various combinations can be arrived at. This technique has been applied effectively to any number of problems and situations. It is only limited by the resourcefulness and imagination of the uses.[6]

## FORCED RELATIONSHIP TECHNIQUE

The simplest form of the *forced relationship technique* is the *catalog method*. It consists merely of opening a catalog, magazine, book, or dictionary and randomly selecting a word, an item, or a subject. The choice of a second word, item, or subject is done in the same arbitrary manner. These elements are then considered together as a means of evoking original thoughts or ideas based on this forced relationship.

Another technique in this category requires listing all the attributes of a problem or situation horizontally. Next, below each

**Table 1**   MATRIX FOR PANELING PROBLEM

| SURFACE APPEARANCE | COLOR OF STAIN | | | |
|---|---|---|---|---|
| | *Maple* | *Walnut* | *Oak* | *Birch* |
| Knotty Wood | Knotty maple | Knotty walnut | Knotty oak | Knotty birch |
| Large Open-Grained | Large open-grained maple | Large open-grained walnut | Large open-grained oak | Large open-grained birch |
| Close-Grained | Close-grained maple | Close-grained walnut | Close-grained oak | Close-grained birch |
| Flecked | Flecked maple | Flecked walnut | Flecked oak | Flecked birch |

### Table 2

| STYLE OF WOOD | COLOR OF STAIN | MATERIAL |
| --- | --- | --- |
| Knotty | Walnut | Plywood |
| Large open-grained | Maple | Wallboard |
| Close-grained | Oak | Hardboard |
| Flecked | Birch | Plastic |

attribute, as many alternatives as can be thought of are listed. The final step consists of making random choices of alternatives from each column. If the forced relationship created does not spark any original and appropriate ideas, the process of random selection is repeated until a novel idea occurs. People who have used this technique claim that after a little practice, new and creative combinations frequently do occur.

## G. POLYA'S CHECKLIST: HOW TO SOLVE IT

The checklist developed by G. Polya, rather than going after a large number of solutions, presents several forms of questioning to define and imaginatively analyze complex or unfamiliar problems. Although designed for mathematical problem solving, this valuable checklist can easily be adapted for problem solving in general.[7]

### Understanding the Problem

*First,* you have to *understand* the problem. What is the unknown? What are the data? What is the condition? Is it possible to satisfy the condition? Is the condition sufficient to determine the unknown? Or is it insufficient? Or redundant? Or contradictory? Draw a figure. Introduce suitable notation. Separate the various parts of the condition. Can you write them down?

### Devising a Plan

*Second, find the connection* between the data and the unknown. You may be obliged to consider auxiliary problems if an immediate connection cannot be found. You should eventually obtain a plan of the solution.

Have you *seen* it before? Or have you seen the same problem in a slightly different form? Do you know a *related problem*? Do you know a theorem that could be useful? Look at the *unknown*! And try to think of a familiar problem having the same or similar unknown. Here is a problem related to yours and solved before. *Could you use it?* Could you use its result? Could you use its method? Should you introduce some auxiliary element in order to make its use possible? Could you *restate* the problem? Could you restate it still differently? Go back to definitions. If you cannot solve the proposed problem, first try to solve some related problem. Could you imagine a more accessible related problem? A more general problem? A more special problem? An analogous problem? Could you solve a part of the problem? Keep only a part of the condition, drop the other part; how far is the unknown then determined, how can it vary? Could you derive something useful from the data? Could you think of other data appropriate to determine the unknown? Could you change the unknown or the data, or both if necessary, so that the new unknown and the new data are nearer to each other? Did you use *all* the data? Did you use the whole condition? Have you taken into account all essential notions involved in the problem?

### Carrying out the Plan

*Third, carry out* your plan. When carrying out your plan of the solution, *check each step.* Can you see clearly that the step is correct? Can you prove that it is correct?

### Looking Back

*Fourth, examine* the solution obtained. Can you *check the result*? Can you check the argument? Can you derive the result differently? Can you see it at a glance? Can you use the result, or the method, for some other problem?

## ROBERT P. INGRAHAM'S IDEASCOPE CHECKLIST

The ideascope checklist was designed to sharpen one's awareness of improvement possibilities and give greater scope to imaginative activity.[8] It consists of eleven basic common goals and objectives:

1. Save time—put time to better use.
2. Save work—make work, labor, or effort more effective.
3. Save material—increase or broaden the use; find a use for supposedly waste material.
4. Make it more understandable.
5. Make it more manageable.
6. Make it safer.
7. Make it healthier.
8. Make it more pleasing and agreeable.
9. Make it more durable.
10. Make it more powerful.
11. Make it more marketable.

After the goal has been decided, Ingraham suggests the use of a list of "action words" to accomplish the purpose by answering the following question:

"What can I _____ (choose appropriate action word(s) from the following list) to accomplish _____ (my goal)?"

### ADD    ADD SOMETHING    SUPPLEMENT IT

By adding a plastic coating over paper twine, rugs were made that resist water, wear, and mildew.

### IMPLEMENT    MAKE A TOOL OR INSTRUMENT

Ball bearings were invented to implement the movement of a wheel, thus reducing friction.

### ADAPT    IMITATE    BORROW

Pasteur heated wine to exactly the right temperature to kill microbes without spoiling the flavor. This idea was applied to milk.

### COMBINE    GROUP    UNITE

Polaroid camera combines picture taking and picture making.

### ARRANGE    REARRANGE    DISTRIBUTE

Eggs at one time were sold in paper bags. Now they are sold in paper cartons, each egg in its own compartment.

### ELIMINATE    EXCLUDE    REJECT

Most organizations today do not send a receipt when a payment is made. This saves time, work, and postage.

*SEPARATE   DIVIDE   DETACH*

Eli Whitney is the founder of mass production by separating labor and standardizing parts. His cotton gin is a separating machine.

*BALANCE   EQUALIZE*

Double entry bookkeeping employs this principle: a debit for every credit.

*REVERSE   INVERT*

H.G. Wells often wrote the last chapter of a novel first to keep the plot from going astray.

*FORM   SHAPE*

Johann Gutenberg gave the world a revolutionary idea with movable type.

*COMPRESS   CONDENSE*

Microelectronics has given us compact computers.

*INDICATE   MAKE UNDERSTANDABLE*

Lectures are now supplanted with participative play-learning systems to make the subject matter to be learned more understandable.

## GENERAL ELECTRIC'S INPUT-OUTPUT SYSTEM

In GE's organized approach to problem solving, a problem is divided into three main groups of desired characteristics, requirements, or objectives.

1. The desired output: clearly spelling out the objectives.
2. The input: defining the starting point or what is available.
3. The limiting conditions: demarcating the conditions under which the output is to be accomplished.[9]

Some of the courses of action that can be taken with this conceptual scheme are:

1. a search for various ways to bridge the gap between input and output;
2. consideration of the many possible ways by which the input might be achieved; and
3. generation of the many alternative ways by which the output might be achieved. This entails a review of all the limiting conditions to establish whether they could be eliminated or substituted for less restrictive conditions.

Example of a typical input-output problem setup for a combination space heater and hair drier:

Output
1. Sufficient quantity of warm air for heating room or drying hair.
2. Meets all requirements of housewife.

Input
1. Electric power for heating element and fan.
2. Manual or automatic control for either one or both.
3. Controls for independently varying temperature and flow of air.

Limiting Conditions
1. Small size.
2. Adaptable portable unit.
3. Lightweight.
4. Noiseless operation.
5. Adaptable to 110 volt AC or DC.
6. Long, trouble-free life.
7. Easily removable parts for repairs if necessary.
8. Low in cost.
9. Easy to keep clean.
10. Attractive appearance.

## JOHN E. ARNOLD'S AREA-THINKING

John E. Arnold developed this list of self-questions at M.I.T. to improve product functions and designs. The list covers four main product features: (1) increased function; (2) higher performance level; (3) lower costs; and (4) increased saleability.

- Can we increase the *function*? Can we make the product do more things?
- Can we get a *higher performance level*? Make the product longer lived? More reliable? More accurate? Safer? More convenient to use? Easier to repair and maintain?
- Can we lower the *cost*? Eliminate excess parts? Substitute cheaper materials? Design to reduce hand labor or for complete automation?
- Can we increase the *saleability*? Improve the appearance of the product? Improve the package? Improve its point of sale?[10]

This area-thinking resembles the checklist technique. The essential difference, however, is that the points to be considered are fewer, broader, and more general. Because of this, greater imaginative play is required to fill in the details.


## DAVIS-HOUTMAN CHECKLIST


Designed primarily for improving or restyling familiar objects, for example, pop-up toasters or shoes, this checklist presents lengthy sublists of possible colors, shapes, alternative ways of rearranging purposes, parts, and functions.[11]

Change Color

| | |
|---|---|
| Blue | Gold |
| Green | Copper |
| Yellow | Brass |
| Orange | Plaid |
| Red | Striped |
| Purple | Polka-dotted |
| White | Flowers |
| Black | Speckles |
| Olive green | Paisley |
| Gray | Pop art |
| Brown | Other Colors |
| Tan | Other color combination |
| Silver | Other patterns |

New Size

| | |
|---|---|
| Longer | Lower |
| Shorter | Larger |
| Wider | Smaller |
| Fatter | Jumbo |
| Thinner | Miniature |
| Thicker | Other size |
| Higher | |

Change Shape

| | |
|---|---|
| Round | Lopsided |
| Square | Sharp corners |
| Triangle | Round corners |
| Oval | Egg-shaped |
| Rectangle | Doughnut-shaped |
| 5-sided | "U"-shaped |
| 6-sided | Other shapes |
| 8-sided | |
| 10-sided | |

### New Material
Plastic
Glass
Fiberglas
Formica
Paper
Wood
Aluminum
Nylon
Cloth

Gunny sack (burlap)
Cardboard
Steel
Leather
Copper
Rubber
Other material
Combination of these materials

### From Other Countries
Oriental
Swedish
Mexican
French
Eskimo

Russian
American
Indian
Egyptian
Spanish

### From Other Styles
Hippie
Beatnik
Other groups
Ivy league

Elves and fairies
Clowns
Football uniform

### From Other Times
Old West
Roaring Twenties
Next Century

Middle Ages
Cave Man
Pioneer

### New Design
Make Stronger
Make Faster
Exaggerate something
Duplicate something

Remove something
Divide
Make lighter
Abbreviate

### Add or Subtract Something
Add new doodad
Add new smell
New sound
New lights

New flavor
New beep beep
New jingle jingle
Subtract the thing that doesn't do anything

### Rearrange things
Switch parts
Change pattern
Combine parts
Other order of operation
Split up

Turn backward
Turn upside down
Turn inside out
Combine purposes
Other switcheroo

## PRODUCT POTENTIAL CHECKLIST

The product potential approach to product analysis serves to high-light the potential capacities of a product and to trigger others that could be incorporated.[12] Additional potentials could affect the use, function, appearance, material, method of manufacturing, market-ability, and so forth.

Following is a list of example products that have been made with the following capacities:

| | |
|---|---|
| Portable | Radios, T.V., typewriters |
| Collapsible | Carriages, chairs, card tables, umbrellas |
| Disposable | Diapers, paper cups, dishes, cigarette lighters |
| Convertible | Cars, coats, sofa beds |
| Reversible | Raincoats, jackets |
| Detachable | Parts of a vacuum cleaner |
| Adjustable | Reclining chairs |
| Returnable | Reuseable containers |
| Renewable | Fillers for ball point pens |
| Retractable | Landing gear, outriggers on field artillery |
| Separable | Camera lenses |
| Flexible | Tools for building and home repair |
| Durable | Polyglycoat car body finish |
| Soluble | Medicine capsules |
| Repairable | Auto body repair |
| Dispensable | Cigarettes, coffee, candy, soft drinks, etc. |
| Mouldable | Putty |
| Compressible | Shock absorbers |
| Edible | Ice cream cones, pie crusts |
| Expandable | Bellows on camera |
| Rotateable | Swivel chairs, revolving doors, turnstiles |

There are many other potentials that can be considered to increase a product's function or use.

## VICE VERSA CHECKLIST

One of the rather odd characteristics of creative people is their readiness to use many opposite associations, images, and concepts when formulating new approaches or solutions to problems. Consideration of opposites encourages new ideas and solutions by loosening one's habitual attitude of taking things for granted or of being satisfied with them the way they are.

Here are some examples of products created by consideration of the opposite form:[13]

| | |
|---|---|
| Short — long | King size cigarettes |
| Round — square | Milk bottles |
| High — low | Ranch-type homes |
| Black — white | White wall tires |
| Solid — hollow | Balloon tires |
| Deep — shallow | Wading pools |
| Sharp — dull | Butter knife |
| Heavy — light | Luggage |
| Thick — thin | Printed circuits |
| Strong — weak | Crash pads, fuses, safety devices |
| Closed — open | Refrigerated display cases |
| Bottom — top | T.V. controls |
| Slow — quick | High-speed movies |
| Stationary — moving | Escalators |
| Hard — soft | Plastic bottles, soft dash boards |
| Manual — powered | Auto brakes, steering, windows |

## SELF-QUESTIONING

If properly done, the answers to the questions What? When? Why? Who? and How? can provide most of the information required on almost any problem. Penetrating and pertinent questions can serve to define a problem properly, to uncover areas where additional information is needed, to establish connections between facts, and to determine the adequacy of a solution. The habit of a questioning attitude and the asking of pertinent questions are vitally important to successful problem solving.

## WORD STIMULATION

Word stimulation constitutes the simplest form of a checklist and usually consists of a list of appropriate words or strategies perused for ideas or suggestions toward a solution. For example, such a list could contain the following words:

| | |
|---|---|
| Adapt | Flow chart |
| Reduce | Guess |
| Expand | Redefine |
| Manipulate | Compile |
| Juxtapose | Relate |
| Organize | Randomize |
| Picture | Repeat |
| Associate | Vary |
| Combine | Change |
| Substitute | Separate |
| Transform | Plan |
| Simulate | Select |
| Symbolize | Record |
| Assume | Visualize |
| Focus | Memorize |
| Question | Display |
| Enlarge | Force |
| Extrapolate | Commit |

Used with intelligence, the techniques in this chapter can stimulate an unimpeded flow of ideas. They can enable problem solvers to get to the rich lode of data deep in their memory storage and bring them to conscious awareness. And as Sidney J. Parnes has pointed out, "If we are able to trigger more of this memory storage into our awareness, we are more likely to make connections that will be productive for us in problem solving."[14]

## REFERENCES

[1] **Alex F. Osborn**, *Applied Imagination.* (New York: Charles Scribner's Sons, 1963).

[2] Ibid.

[3] **Robert P. Crawford**, *Techniques of Creative Thinking.* (New York: Hawthorn Books, Inc., 1954).

[4] Cited in "Creativity and Problem Solving," (monograph mimeod), Southern Bell Tel: Tel. Co., Atlanta, Ga., February 1964, pp. 102-3.

[5] **Kenneth L. Pittman**, "Morphological Analysis and Speculation," in Angelo M. Biondi, ed., *Have an Affair with Your Mind.* (New York: Creative Synergetic Associates, Ltd., 1974), p. 38.

[6] Ibid., p. 40.

[7] G. **Polya,** How To Solve It. (Princeton, N.J.: Princeton University Press, 1973), pp. xvi–xvii.

[8] **Robert P. Ingraham,** "Ideascope," (monograph), 1962, p. 29.

[9] "AC Notes on Creativity," (monograph), AC Spark Plug Division of General Motors Corp.

[10] **John E. Arnold,** "AC Notes on Creativity."

[11] **G.A. Davis** and **S.E. Houtman,** "Thinking Creatively: A Guide to Training Imagination," Wisconsin Research and Development Center for Cognitive Learning, University of Wisconsin, 1968.

[12] Arnold, "AC Notes on Creativity."

[13] Ibid.

[14] **Sidney J. Parnes,** "Idea-Stimulation Techniques," *Journal of Creative Behavior,* 10 (second quarter, 1976), no. 2. p. 129.

# 5

# ENHANCING CREATIVITY THROUGH SYNECTICS

One of the most promising innovative approaches to creativity and problem solving is synectics (from a Greek word that means the fitting together of diverse elements).

The method was devised by Synectics, Inc., of Cambridge, Massachusetts. This organization is presently working in four areas: (1) invention of products and processes for sale or license to industry; (2) consulting with client companies on specific problems; (3) teaching the Synectics method to groups of industrial and business personnel; (4) continuing research into the creative process.

Study of the thought processes of highly creative people has shown that they have the ability to see problems in new and previously unthought-of ways. They stress the "nonrational" aspects of creativity, using analogies that provide novel contexts for approaching a problem with a fresh outlook. Synectics has adopted this and deliberately cultivates and makes use of the seemingly irrelevant.

## TEN IMPORTANT PRINCIPLES

The following ten principles of Synectics are considered essential to creative problem solving:[1]

1. Proceed on the assumption that things are possible. (British author Arthur C. Clarke has said, "When a distinguished but elderly scientist states that something is possible, he is almost certainly right. Where he states that something is impossible, he is very probably wrong. . . . Recent history is full of incidents in which highly knowledgeable individuals have flatly denied the feasibility of some development, which before long turned out to be quite practicable. For example, the great atomic theory pioneer, Lord Rutherford, insisted that it was impossible to harness nuclear energy."[2] )

2. Isolate fixed ideas and overcome them.

3. Do not search for solutions, but for new ways to view the problem.

4. Seize on tentative, half-formed possibilities.

5. Recognize that new ideas (one's own as well as others') are fragile, and listen positively to them.

6. Entertain the apparently unthinkable.

7. Articulate the apparently unspeakable.

8. Defer conclusions until a number of variables have been floated.

9. Keep track (by means of brief notation) of the process.

10. Enjoy it!

## CREATIVE POTENTIAL

George M. Prince, president of Synectics, Inc., believes that in order for people to use more of their creative potential, they have to combat and change the strangling effect of their education and be more open to life's experiences. He goes on to say, "This has obvious implications for traditional education and business. We believe these are not so much bad as they are incomplete. An important part of us is ignored both in training and on the job. Because our emotional and imaginative elements are as much a part of us as our intellect or our bodies, this neglect produces a discomfort and uneasiness. We believe that business pays a high penalty for a structure and tradition that leaves such a vital component of its people unused. . . . You must be convinced by evidence you feel and observe, that it is in your best interest to entertain and encourage your intuitions, your desires and your daydreams."[3]

Dr. Lawrence Kubie, a psychiatrist, has emphasized the great importance of free play and toying in one's thinking if one wants to enhance his or her creative problem-solving processes:

> Whence then comes our creative function? To answer this we have to stop for a moment to indicate what we mean by creativity. Clearly, by the creative process we mean the capacity to find new and unexpected connections, to voyage freely over the seas, to happen on America as we seek new routes to India, to find new relationships in time and space, and thus new meanings. Or to put it in another way, it means working freely with conscious and preconscious metaphor, with slang, puns, overlapping meanings, and figures of speech, with vague similarities, with the reminiscent recollections evoked by some minute ingredients of experience, establishing links to something else which in other respects may be quite different. It is free in the sense that it is not anchored either to the pedestrian realities of our conscious symbolic processes, or to the rigid symbolic relationships of the unconscious areas of personality. This is precisely why the free play of preconscious symbolic processes is vital for all creative productivity.[4]

## ENHANCING CREATIVITY

Synectics research has indicated that the commodity called creativity is much more universally distributed among the population than is usually supposed. It has also been noted that the creative habit can be reawakened in people who seem to have lost it, and strengthened in people who regularly display it.

Synectics training seeks to increase the creative capacity of each participant through (1) developing a greater understanding of creative thought processes, and (2) improving the ability, consciously and deliberately, to make use of creative mechanisms.

In order to achieve the goals, the Synectics group has adopted procedures that lead to imaginative speculation and modes of behavior that encourage and value speculation. Of speculation Prince says, "Free speculation and disciplined reaction to it [are] of urgent importance, for there is a relentless gravity-like force working against speculation. This force is dangerous especially because it is so easily justified as realistic thinking. . . . Each of us pays convincing lip service to his willingness—even eagerness—to consider new thoughts and ideas. But 1,000 tapes, such as we [Synectics, Inc.] have made, make liars of us all. People use remarkable ingenuity to make clear by tone, nonverbal slights, tuning out, helpful criticism, false issues, and outright negativity that they are not only against ideas and change, but also against those who propose it. We humans habitually try to protect ourselves even from our own new ideas."[5]

The Synectics procedures were developed through the aid of the tape recorder and video tape. Hundreds of meetings of different groups of people (usually from five to seven) were analyzed and clues to the kinds of thinking that produce new ideas were documented. Experiments with various procedures finally enabled the Synectics groups to come up with various operational mechanisms that have proved most productive.

## OPERATIONAL MECHANISMS OF SYNECTICS

### Goal as Understood

The *goal as understood* is, according to Prince, "a formalization of a step in the natural problem-solving process."[6] To understand a problem, participants must first relate it to known things or experiences. Imaginative solutions are then sought to fulfill the demands of the problem.

Participants are urged to wish for anything imaginable, even if it violates laws known to be true. Real world restrictions are later considered before a final viewpoint is accepted. As the participant's skill increases, the imagined solutions become more wishful. Even though these may seem less possible to obtain, they are more useful as goals as understood.

Each participant is urged to create one or more goals as understood. These are then listed for the entire group to see. According to Prince, this allows each member to make the problem his or her own: "We found in our research that each person has his own ways of seeing problems. He apparently cannot agree with another's specific statement without serious reservation. There is no reason why he should. He is there because you want to use his mind. His personal statement of the goal or problem will certainly be useful to him and it may be evocative to the whole group. In our culture there is, in chairmen, an urge to get consensus of the problem to be worked on. We believe consensus at this point is not only impossible (it seems to violate some basic law of individuality), it is undesirable. If the members understand there are different views of the problem and that these differences are useful and will be recorded, each can relax about his own slightly different view and stop trying to make converts."[7]

## Making the Strange Familiar

The two basic approaches in the Synectics process are making the strange familiar and making the familiar strange. The first of these is the analytical phase, which plumbs the ramifications and the fundamentals of the problem to get at the heart of it. Making the strange familiar is essentially congenial to the natural tendency of the mind. When presented with a problem, or with something unfamiliar, the natural tendency is to convert it into manageable familiarity through analysis and comparison with previously consolidated information and data.

The three basic procedures employed in making the strange familiar are analysis, generalization, and model-seeking. Analysis involves reducing the problem into its component parts in order to see the forest more clearly by identifying the individual trees. Generalization is the process of identifying significant patterns among the component parts. By model-seeking, the formulation of generalizations is facilitated.

Although analysis is a necessary part of creative problem solving, it is full of pitfalls. Often it involves mere concentration on details that become ends in themselves, leading one into a variety of superficial solutions. "It helps, therefore," says Prince, "to encourage people to air their immediate solutions and to discuss them fully. Even if these ideas are not destined for adoption, the expert's explanations of their virtues and flaws will help the group to under-stand the problem."[8]

Analysis, in itself, does not lead one into a fresh viewpoint or into a new way of looking at the problem. For this, the approach of making the familiar strange is necessary.

## Making the Familiar Strange

Through the deliberate distortion, inversion, or transposition, the everyday habitual ways of looking at things are rendered strange. It is not merely a search for the bizarre or out-of-the-way, it is a con-scious attempt to achieve a new look at the familiar world and to transpose our usual ways of perceiving and our habitual expectations about how we or the world will behave.

Synectics emphasizes the importance of viewpoints and claims that a usefully strange viewpoint can suggest several different poten-tial solutions. While the traditional problem-solving procedures seek solutions, Synectics seeks new viewpoints, using them as spring-boards to solution.

Synectics has adopted three mechanisms for making the familiar strange: (1) personal analogy or example, (2) direct analogy, and (3) symbolic analogy or "book title."

*Personal Analogy*   In Synectics, personal analogy involves using one's own highly personal emotions, feelings, and characteristics for obtaining insight into problems. As Prince explains, "One identifies oneself with a purely nonhuman entity which figures in the problem, investing it with one's own vitality, speculating on how that thing would 'feel' and act in the problem situation. This device has proven an invaluable tool for making the familiar strange. Personal identifi-cation with the elements of a problem releases the individual from viewing the problem in terms of its previously analyzed elements."[9]

According to Synectics, there are three degrees of involvement in personal analogy:[10]

1. First-person description of facts.

*Leader's Question:* You are a tuning fork. How do you feel?

*Response:* I am made of metal and have very precise dimen-sions. When struck, I vibrate at a fixed frequency.

This is a shallow personal analogy, for it only gives analytical facts recited in the first person.

2. First-person description of emotions.

*Leader's Question:* You are a tuning fork. How do you feel?

*Response:* I feel sensitive but only to very special things. You can hit me with a hammer and I don't care at all, but if you whistle just the right note, I feel I am going all to pieces.

This is a good translation of analytical facts into feelings.

3. Empathic identification with the subject.

*Leader's Question:* You are a tuning fork. How do you feel?

*Response:* My nerves are shot. Here I am, a high-grade piece of steel, and when the right tone sounds, I have a breakdown! But I am intensely responsible and narrow-minded. Dead to anything until my frequency comes around and then, WOW!

This response is the most interesting and suggestive.

*Personal Analogy: An Example* A Synectics group had been attacking a problem of inventing a new and inexpensive constant-speed mechanism: How to run a shaft at input speeds varying from 400 to 4,000 rpm, so that the power take-off end of this shaft always turns at 400? Since many many competent engineers had tried to solve this constant-speed problem, there was little hope for arriving at anything elegant unless a totally new viewpoint was gained.

A mechanism for making this familiar problem strange was personal analogy. A sketch was drawn on the blackboard showing a box with a shaft entering and going out. The entering shaft was labeled "400 to 4,000"; the exiting shaft was labeled "400 constant." One after the other, each member of the group "entered" the box and attempted to effect with his own body the constant speed required. Here are some excerpts from the recorded session in response to the question: "You're in the box—how to you feel? What do you do?"

*Response 1.* Okay, I'm in the black box. I grab the in-shaft with one hand and grab the out-shaft with the other. I let the in-shaft slip when I think it's going too fast so that the out-shaft will stay constant. . . .

*Response 2.* Well, my hands are getting . . . too hot to hold I guess . . . at least one hand, that is . . . the one that's acting like a clutch . . . slipping.

*Response 3.* I'm in the box and I am trying to be a governor . . . to be a feedback system . . . built in . . . let's see, if I grab the out-shaft with my hands . . . and let's say there's a plate on the in-shaft so that my feet can press against it. . . . I put my feet way out in the periphery of the plate and . . . what I would like is for my feet to get smaller as the speed of the in-shaft increases because then the friction would be reduced and I would hold on to the out-shaft for dear life and its speed might remain constant. . . . The faster the in-shaft went the smaller my feet would become so that the driving force would stay the same.[11]

The analogies given above not only increase the understanding of the problem, they also suggest potential avenues of solution.

*Direct Analogy*  This mechanism is used to compare parallel facts, knowledge, or technology. The procedure entails searching one's experiences and knowledge to marshal phenomena that have some similar relationships with the problem at hand. However, exact comparisons or comparisons with subject matter too close to the problem are useless for the purpose of making the familiar strange. For example, comparing an organ with a piano is too close a parallel to evoke new viewpoints; comparing it with a typewriter might produce more intriguing notions.

In the case of technical problems, analogies are drawn from the organic world. Comparisons from different areas of exact science, on the other hand, tend to be too close. The following example of a direct analogy illustrates the value of organic comparisons.

*Example of Direct Analogy*  A Synectics group was attempting to solve the problem of how to invent a new kind of roof that would be more actively serviceable than traditional roofs. Analysis of the problem indicated that there might be an economic advantage in having a roof that is white in the summer and black in the winter. The white roof would reflect the sun's rays in the summer so that the cost of air conditioning could be reduced. The black roof would absorb heat in the winter so that the cost of heating could be minimized. The following are some direct analogy examples from the session on this problem, which started with the question: "What in nature changes color?"

*Response 1.* A weasel—white in winter, brown in summer; camouflage. It's not voluntary and the weasel only changes color twice a year. . . . I think our roof should change color with the heat of the sun. . . . There are hot days in the spring and fall . . . cold ones too.

*Response 2.* A flounder turns white if he is over white sand and then he turns dark if he lands on black sand. In a flounder the color changes from dark to light and light to dark. . . . I shouldn't say "color," because although a bit of brown and yellow comes out, the flounder doesn't have any blue or red in his register. . . . Anyway, this changing is partly voluntary and partly involuntary where a reflex action automatically adapts to the surrounding conditions. This is how the switching works: In the deepest layer of its skin are black-pigmented chromatophores—balls of color. When these are pushed toward the surface the flounder is covered with black spots so that he looks black . . . like an impressionistic painting where a whole bunch of little dabs of paint give the appearance of total covering. Only when you get up close to a Seurat can you see the little atomistic dabs. When the black pigment withdraws to the bottom of these chromatophores, then the flouder appears light colored. . .

*Analysis.* Let's compare the flounder analogy to the roof problem. Let's say we make up a roofing material that's black, except buried in the black stuff are little white plastic balls. When the sun comes out and the roof gets hot the little white balls expand according to Boyle's Law. They pop through the black roofing vehicle. Now the roof is white, impressionistically white, that is, à la Seurat. Just like the flounder, only with reverse English. Is it the black pigmented part of the chromatophores that come to the surface of the flounder's skin? OK, in our roof it will be the white pigmented plastic balls that come to the surface when the roof gets hot. There are many ways to think about this.

Over a period of years Synectics research has observed that perhaps the richest source of direct analogy is biology. This is because the language of biology lacks a mystifying terminology, and the organic aspect of biology brings out analogies that breathe life into problems that are stiff and rigidly quantitative.

*Symbolic Analogy*   As defined by Synectics, symbolic analogy is a "highly compressed, almost poetic, statement of the implications of a key word selected from the goal as understood or having some connection with the problem."

George M. Prince explains the mechanism of symbolic analogy or "book title" this way:

> The procedure is to select the key word and ask yourself (or a member of your group) for the essence of its meaning to you. Empathize or feel for the important connotations of the word. Then try to put those feelings

into one or two words. The more general or all-encompassing these words are, the more potentially useful in suggesting areas for speculation. Straight definitions are not useful because they are low level descriptions of a one-to-one type. They give little opportunity to search for associations. In a Synectics session directed toward detecting the presence of an unwanted flame in a piece of sophisticated hardware, the question was asked: "What is the essence of flameness?"

*Response 1.* (Thinking to self) "A flame is ghostly and seems insubstantial but is very much there . . . it's a ghostly thereness."

*Response 2.* "It's ghostly because it wavers and doesn't seem to have much substance but if you put your finger in its territory it sure is there."

*Response 3.* "It really does occupy that space and nothing else can. . . . It's a ghost with a shell."

*Response 4.* "Or a skin, or a wall . . . a ghostly wall."[12]

Considering a flame as a ghostly wall led to some rewarding lines of speculation.

These symbolic analogies, or "book titles" as they are sometimes called, are difficult to create; the crucial essence of a subject must be compressed into a single meaningful phrase. However, people trained in Synectics claim that this mechanism leads more often to conceptual breakthroughs than any of the others described. The "useful strangeness" that is imparted to familiar objects and concepts transcends that which can be obtained by the use of either personal or direct analogy.

Following are some typical symbolic analogies with the key words to which they apply listed at the left:

| | |
|---|---|
| ratchet | dependable intermittency |
| viscosity | hesitant displacement |
| solidity | enforced togetherness |
| forest fire | progressive ingestion |
| machine-gun burst | connected pauses |
| target | focused desire |
| mixture | balanced confusion |
| multitude | discreet infinity |
| acid | impure aggressor |
| receptivity | involuntary willingness |

## Analogies: Their Importance

The analogical mechanisms are the most important part of the Synectics method, although they often appear ambiguous and irrelevant.

Prince, in defense of the ambiguity, says, "It is this very ambiguity on which Synectics depends for making the familiar strange. But the analogies must be sought within an ordered framework if they are to be efficient. And they must be 'force-fitted' to the problem if they are to be effective. This is the most difficult of the Synectics procedures. Through the strain of this new fit, the problem is stretched and pulled and refocused in order that it may be seen in a new way. If no deliberate attempt is made to find relevance in apparent irrelevance, then one analogy can merely lead to another and another, and potentially fruitful viewpoints will be bypassed."[13]

## SYNECTICS FLOWCHART

The various mechanisms used by the Synectics group to increase speculation on the part of participants must be arranged in some manner before they can be useful in reaching a comprehensive, creative solution. In order to impose a disciplined framework on the generation, development, and use of logical mechanisms, Synectics, Inc., has developed the following flowchart upon which all sessions are constructed.[14]

## GOALS AS UNDERSTOOD

The manner in which the problem is stated significantly influences the manner in which the problem is approached. Therefore, following the statement of the problem as given, there is an analytical phase during which the group decides which formulation of the problem is to be the first subject of attack. Their choice becomes the goal as understood.

This analytical stage accomplishes a number of purposes. It acquaints participants with the problem and its background. It also elicits and nullifies immediate solution possibilities, which inevitably arise but which rarely prove adequate. An individual's constructive participation in the session is lost as long as he dwells on the first solution possibility. Therefore, it is essential that all members purge themselves of premature solutions as they arise.

---

### SYNECTICS FLOWCHART

A. Problem as given—form a general statement of the problem to be solved.

B. Analyze and discuss the problem—make the strange familiar. Expert analyzes and explains the problem.

C. Purge all immediate solutions.

D. Goal as understood—select an element or aspect of the problem upon which to concentrate.

E. Leader's (evocative) question—the leader devises a question that forces an analogical answer by:

    1. Direct analogy (example),

    2. Personal analogy, or

    3. Symbolic analogy (book title)

F. Play with the analogy to understand all its implications.

G. Apply this understanding to the goal as understood (or problem as given) to see if a new viewpoint can be developed.

H. Pursue one of the following courses:

    1. If there is a new viewpoint, develop it as far as possible and then evaluate it.

    2. If there is no new viewpoint, begin another "excursion" to make the familiar strange.

        a. Make more analogies for the same leader's question and repeat steps F and G, or

        b. Return to the goal as understood, form a new leader's question, and repeat steps F and G, or

        c. If the work in step G reveals a new aspect to the problem, state this as a new goal as understood and repeat steps E, F, and G.

---

The first goal as understood merely serves as a common starting point, judged by the group as a potentially fruitful topic upon which to concentrate. The goal as understood is frequently restated, and it is not uncommon for the group to discover that the real heart of the problem is not effectively defined by the problem as given.

## ANALOGICAL ROUTE

After the goal as understood is formulated, the group leader must decide which analogical route the group is to take. He does this using the criterion of "constructive psychological strain." With a mechanical problem, for example, he would look for biological models; with people-oriented problems he might seek analogies from the exact sciences. Synectics groups have found that the more concrete the problem, the more likely is a symbolic analogy fruitful.

The leader evokes analogical responses by means of evocative questions which form the bridge between analysis and analogy. He or she specifies which type of analogy is wanted (direct, personal, or symbolic) and usually solicits the response from a particular group member. Each group member has a greater facility with one type of analogy as compared with another. The experienced leader soon learns which analogies are most natural to each member, and he or she capitalizes on it.

## ANALOGY DEVELOPMENT

After the analogy has emerged, the group devotes all its attention to it and defers, for the time being, all conscious thought of the problem as given. In the subconscious, however, the problem as given acts as a guide to signal the group members whenever a useful viewpoint implied by the analogies is articulated.

A period of analogy development ensues, during which all the details of the analogy are analyzed and the important details emphasized. If the group fails to articulate a useful connection between the goal as understood and the analogy, the leader directs them to try a "force-fitting" connection, ensuring that all potential viewpoints from the analogy are considered.

If the analogy succeeds in illuminating the goal as understood, a viewpoint is gained, and an attempt is made to apply it to the problem as given to see if it fulfills all requirements of the problem. If it fails to do so, a new goal as understood is stated. This statement reflects the questions that were left unanswered or the difficulties that were encountered. If the analogy fails to move the new goal as understood closer to solution, a new analogical exercise is required.

## THE GROUP LEADER

Although the Synectics group sessions are conducted by a leader, his or her functions are different from what is usually implied by the term. The Synectics leader never judges the merits of a contribution. Neither does he or she act as a moderator or a chairman. The leader's major function is to see that problem investigation stays within the confines of the flowchart. This also ensures the most efficient generation, development, and use of analogies. In a sense, the leader's role is often that of merely filling in the gaps "between speeches" and of keeping track of the progress on boards or easel pads for review by participants.

## Pathological Optimism

An important quality in a leader, according to William J.J. Gordon, is "an almost pathological optimism supporting a refusal to give up." He goes on to point out that, "Solutions to many problems remain undiscovered because inventors run out of creative energy just when they are on the brink. Of course, it is impossible to know where the brink is, but in the case of all problems, there exist certain walls which define the line where others have surrendered. It is just when we strike these seemingly impenetrable bastions that we tend toward despair, like others before us . . . and it is then that we are on the verge of solution. We all know the feeling of suddenly being conceptually let down. We think hard and long about something and then collapse. . . . With group participants thinking along the same general lines, since everybody does not let down at the same time, the conceptual energy which has built up is kept in play."[15]

## Wise Use of Power

Wise leaders do not compete with their teams. They should, indeed, refrain from contributing any ideas of their own. Experience has shown that when they do offer ideas, the members' contributions and free-wheeling ideation are materially reduced. Only when no ideas are forthcoming in the early "suggestion" and "force fit" stages of the process should leaders offer ideas to get the proceedings moving again.

Effective leaders support the ideas offered by the members and restate them to crystallize understanding. They may build upon or add to these ideas, but at all times the others' ideas are given precedence over the leader's ideas. Leaders should be extraordinarily good listeners, and through playback and restatements, prove that they have understood what the members have contributed. This constructive stance has a liberating effect on the group, and it creates the feeling in the members that all notions and ideas are welcome and worthwhile, no matter how farfetched or hazy they might seem.

## Intervening Without Manipulating

In order to encourage each group member to give his or her own unique response to the various questions, the leader must handle each person with care. One of the tools is the *intraverbal phrase,* a statement that encourages a direction without imposing constraints or narrowing its scope. Following is a list of some intraverbals suggested by Prince:[16]

- OK.
- What you want to do, if I get you, is. . .
- Good, yes?
- Do you have an idea how to do that?
- What would you like to be? (looking for information)
- Great.
- How about that? What is your feeling about that? (direct to expert)
- Any other thoughts about this?
- I'd like you to work it. . .
- What about that? (to expert)
- What is particularly useful about. . . ?
- What is your concern about this?
- Can we draw something out of this?
- What is appealing about that?
- Would you write a goal based on that? (slight change in subject)
- This is very useful.
- I am not sure. Let me hear. (bring out bashful ideas)
- Let's wish for the real thing.
- Good. Great. The more difference the better.
- Wait a minute. (slow speaker down)
- What is your reaction?
- Let's put that one down. (new goal)
- That is the kind of solution I like because. . .
- Very interesting.
- Say more about it. (draw out idea)
- Anybody feel differently? (personal analogy)
- What comes to your mind?
- I want just anything at all that comes to your mind. (examine)
- It's fine. (reassurance)
- Is there some way we could use this so that. . .(overcome objection)

- You have an idea. How might we do that?
- What would you like it to be?
- Can we improve on this?
- Write it down. (when someone interrupts with new idea)
- How should I word this? (to expert)
- Tell me more.
- What do you like about this?
- What's on your mind?
- Tell us about it—we don't care.
- Is there some way we could use this? (and turn it around)
- Keep talking.
- I love the idea that . . . but can we add to that by. . .
- How can we use this idea?
- That's an interesting notion, what do you think?
- Why don't you put the meanings to the words that you like.
- How about that?
- What specifically is implied there that you like? What concerns you about it?
- Could you phrase that as a goal?
- I'd like you to word it in such a way that it directs us to do something.
- What would make this more effective?
- Can you give me some words? (in writing a goal or possible solution)
- What is appealing about that?
- I think I've got you. How can we put that? (discourages person from monopolizing the conversation)
- Can we go on?
- Can we do any more with this? If not, shall we make it into a goal?
- Anything goes here.
- I have the feeling that here is a marvelous goal. If no one has a solution, I'd like to put it up.
- How can we turn that into a goal and keep all the plusses?
- Rather than raise a philosophical question, can you word it as a goal so we can do something about it?
- What are you thinking?
- What is your reaction?
- Have you got it written down?
- What is bothering you?
- What you said is very desirable.
- If I get what you want to do is. . .(making sure you understand)
- This notion is very valuable because. . .
- Sounds as if it might be a possible solution.
- Can you wish for something?
- Would you like to address a goal to a bigger problem?
- Maybe we can build on that.

## GROUP MEMBERS

One factor that is crucial to the success of the Synectics group is diversity. The individuals selected (five to seven in addition to the leader) should represent divergent backgrounds, training, and experience. The first benefit gained from this diversity is the ability of each participant to view the problem from a different perspective. It is extremely difficult for an individual to step back from a deep understanding of, or familiarity with, a problem in order to look at it afresh. A diverse group can do this much more readily. The second benefit is the variety of knowledge that can be brought to bear on the problem. As Dean L. Gitter says, "The possibilities of innovation are greatest in the no-man's land which separates specialties, rather than in the well-trodden areas within specific fields."[17]

## DESTRUCTIVE IMPACT OF CRITICISM

The Synectics group takes particular pains to show the members of the group the destructive consequences of negative reactions and criticism, even though they may claim that they are, as mature individuals, immune to criticism. As Prince says,

> Negative reactions and feelings are difficult to handle. No one wants to think of himself as a negative person who kills ideas before they have a chance to develop. So none of us thinks of himself in this way. With the rationale that it is constructive to do so, much of our analytical training has taught us to react critically to the ideas of both ourselves and our fellows: "If I see something wrong with an idea, why shouldn't I point it out? What's the use of developing a bad idea?" So goes the argument, and often with it go the chances that a new and potentially successful idea will be developed.
>
> . . .Bad habits of unnecessary precision, censorship, and anxiety about the regard of others have made nearly all of us ignorant of our own capabilities. The human animal is the only one on earth so intelligent that it can actually learn to be stupid."[18]

## MEASURED EFFECT OF ANTAGONISM

In an attempt to obtain some measurement of the effect of seemingly mild antagonism, the Synectics group experimented with a psychogalvanometer, a device that measures changes in skin resistance. Electrodes were attached to two fingers of a subject, and the pointer was brought to a normal reading. One of the experimenters then told the subject in a quiet tone, "I am not upset or anything, but I'm going to gently slap your arm." The subject's arm was given a gentle slap. In about fifteen seconds the pointer rose sharply. Later, in meeting with the subject, they waited until he proposed an idea. The act of voicing an idea made the pointer climb, suggesting some emotional involvement. When the pointer settled down, they used a familiar cliché, "I hate to be negative, but, . . ." and they found some fault with the subject's idea. He remained outwardly calm and reasonable, but the pointer jumped as if they had slapped him.

To overcome the bad habits of compulsive criticism and negative reactions, Prince makes the following suggestion: "We have repeatedly observed that in the early stages of an emerging idea, no one can know with certainty that a flaw is in fact fatal. Because it seems to be universal that the faults in an idea will take precedence in your mind, don't fight it; simply do not voice the faults. Comfort yourself with the silent promise that you will get to them in good time. Then temporarily focus the very best of you—your intellect, your feelings, your intuitions—on that small spectrum of the idea that is worthwhile. Talk about it."[19]

## THE IMPORTANCE OF LISTENING

The ability to listen effectively is considered one of the most vital of skills. Therefore, Synectics devotes a considerable amount of time teaching it to group members. As Prince states, "Most of our behavioral models, such as parents and teachers, are typically bad listeners. Listening is usually seen as trying to figure out as quickly as possible what is the gist of another person's message. The gist is carefully screened by an individual's preconceptions. He then tunes out and prepares his own official statement on the subject he assumes is under discussion. Once you have become a skilled listener, you will observe that it is more the rule than the exception that people talk at one another rather than with one another."[20]

## A Listening Exercise

The renowned psychologist Carl Rogers has made an exhaustive investigation of the role that poor listening plays in interpersonal communication. He suggests the following exercise for people to test the quality of their understanding:

I would like to propose, as an hypothesis for consideration, that the major barrier to mutual interpersonal communication is our very natural tendency to judge, to evaluate, to approve or disapprove, the statement of the other person, or the other group. Let me illustrate my meaning with some very simple examples. As you leave the meeting tonight, one of the statements you are likely to hear is, "I didn't like that man's talk." Now what do you respond? Almost invariably your reply will be either approval or disapproval of the attitude expressed. Either you respond, "I didn't either. I thought it was terrible," or else you tend to reply, "Oh, I thought it was really good." In other words, your primary reaction is to evaluate what has just been said to you, to evaluate it from *your* point of view, your own frame of reference. . . .The tendency to react to any emotionally meaningful statement by forming an evaluation of it from our own point of view, is, I repeat, the major barrier to interpersonal communication. But is there any way of solving this problem of avoiding this barrier? I feel that we are making exciting progress toward this goal and I would like to present it as simply as I can. Real communication occurs, and this evaluation tendency is avoided, when we listen with understanding. What does that mean? It means to see the expressed idea and attitude from the other person's point of view, to sense how it feels to him, to achieve his frame of reference in regard to the thing he is talking about. Some of you may be feeling that you listen well to people, and that you have never seen . . . results. The chances are very great indeed that your listening has not been of the type I have described. Fortunately I can suggest a . . . laboratory experiment which you can try to test the quality of your understanding. The next time you get into an argument with your wife, or your friend, or with a small group of friends, just stop the discussion for a moment and for an experiment, institute this rule. "Each person can speak up for himself only *after* he has first restated the ideas and feelings of the previous speaker accurately, and to that speaker's satisfaction." You see what this would mean. It would . . . mean that before presenting your own point of view, it would be necessary for you to really achieve the other speaker's frame of reference—to understand his thoughts and feelings so well that you could summarize them for him. Sounds simple, doesn't it? But if you try it you will discover it one of the most difficult things you have ever tried to do. However, once you have been able to see the other's point of view, your own comments will have to be drastically revised. You will also find the emotion going out of the discussion, the differences being reduced, and those differences which remain being of a rational and understandable sort.

I have said that our research and experience to date would make it appear that breakdowns in communication, and the evaluative tendency which is the major barrier to communication, can be avoided. The solution is provided by creating a situation in which each of the different parties comes to understand the other from the *other's* point of view. This has been achieved, in practice, even when feelings run high, by the influence of a person who is willing to understand each point of view empathically, and who thus acts as a catalyst to precipitate further understanding. This procedure has important characteristics. It can be initiated by one party, without waiting for the other to be ready. It can even be initiated by a neutral third person, providing he can gain a minimum of cooperation from one of the parties. This procedure can deal with the insincerities, the defensive exaggerations, the lies, the "false fronts" which characterize almost every failure in communication. These defensive distortions drop away with astonishing speed as people find that the only intent is to understand, not judge. This approach leads steadily and rapidly toward the discovery of the truth, toward a realistic appraisal of the objective barriers to communication. The dropping of some defensiveness by one party leads to further dropping of defensiveness by the other party, and truth is thus approached.[21]

The Synectics group has applied Dr. Rogers' work on mutual listening to their problem-solving meetings. This practice has proven most useful in the early stages of developing a solution. Participants set aside their usual critical, analytical urges and try to understand fully the new idea with its rich ambiguities and incompleteness. In this way, they can more readily perceive the intentions, feelings, intuitions, and even hopes that lie behind the spoken words.

## FORMING A SYNECTICS GROUP

Dean L. Gitter feels that companies interested in establishing Synectics groups in their companies should assemble a group of men and women who have worked in various areas of the company's activities—production, research, finance, sales, development, and so forth. This makes it possible to maximize the knowledge of the company's needs, opportunities, and attitudes and to break through the arbitrary barriers that inevitably exist between the various divisions and departments of a corporation. As Gitter says, "If we combine in one group knowledge of possibilities extant in the marketplace, basic research knowledge which has yet to be capitalized on, practical abilities to unite these poles, and an over-all commitment to get the job done, then the possibility exists for synthesizing both an inventor and entrepreneur out of the individual possessing these skills."[22]

The groups trainded by Synectics, Inc., are exposed to a variety of problems that are usually supplied by management. These problems must be of immediate importance to the company in order to elicit the group's interest and dedication. The problem should also be of sufficient potential profitability to assuage management's perennial concern with the expenditures of time and energies.

### Group Commando Tactics

The first few problems attacked by the group should lend themselves to short-range implementation and quantifiable results. This gives the group a sense of achievement and a faith in the newly learned *modus operandi* of Synectics.

An early solution is often used as a "scapegoat," according to Dean L. Gitter. "By this I mean that we have found it useful to deliberately sacrifice one of the group's early inventions, to send it out into the organization and observe the direction from which the arrows come to shoot it down, and the techniques the hunters use to do it. In watching this slaughter, the group learns many things which it can correct in the future; it develops a heightened sense of the reliance they must place on each other . . . it begins to evolve a set of commando tactics for coping with opposition. Above all, it begins to find its own sense of style and the satisfaction which comes from commitment."[23]

## SOLO SYNECTICS

Although the Synectics mechanisms were developed primarily for group use, they can also be used profitably for individual problem solving. A New York executive performs a paper and pencil Synectics session every morning during his hour-long trip to the office. Like many other skills, problem-solving techniques can be improved with practice, according to Gitter. "Hundreds of individuals'who have consciously used the mechanisms of Synectics report that they are mentally more limber in dealing with problems. Ideas come more easily; they see possibilities where before they did not. In short, like an athlete in shape, they feel more confident of their problem-solving capability."[24]

## REFERENCES

[1] Dean L. Gitter, "Creative Sparks to Kindle Oil Industry," *Petroleum Management*, April 1965, p. 94.

[2] Eugene Raudsepp, "Synectics: Enhancing Group Creativity—Part 1," *Hydrocarbon Processing*, December 1970, p. 105.

[3] George M. Prince, *The Practice of Creativity*. (Cambridge, Mass.: Synectics, Inc., 1969), p. 23.

[4] Lawrence S. Kubie, *Neurotic Distortion of the Creative Process*. (New York: The Noonday Press, 1961), p. 141.

[5] Prince, *Practice*, p. xii.

[6] Ibid., p. 93.

[7] Ibid., p. 94.

[8] Eugene Raudsepp, "Forcing Ideas with Synectics," *Machine Design*, October 16, 1969, p. 135.

[9] Ibid., pp. 135-36.

[10] William J.J. Gordon, *Synectics*. (New York: Harper & Row Publishers, Inc., 1961), pp. 38-39.

[11] Raudsepp, "Synectics", p. 107.

[12] Raudsepp, "Forcing Ideas," p. 137.

[13] Ibid., pp. 137-38.

[14] Eugene Raudsepp, "Synectics: Enhancing Group Creativity—Part II," *Hydrocarbon Processing*, January 1971, pp. 133-34.

[15] Raudsepp, "Synectics: Enhancing Group Creativity—Part 2," p. 135.

[16] Raudsepp, "Forcing Ideas," pp. 135-36.

[17] Gitter, "Creative Sparks," p. 95.

[18] Raudsepp, "Forcing Ideas," p. 137.

[19] Ibid.

[20] Ibid.

[21] Carl R. Rogers, "Communication: Its Blocking and Its Facilitation," *Northwestern University Information*, 20 (April 22, 1952), no. 25.

[22] Gitter and Raudsepp, "Synectics: Enhancing Group Creativity—Part II," p. 139.

[23] Ibid., p. 139.

[24] Ibid., p. 139.

# 6

# THE VALUE
# OF INTUITIVE THINKING

One of the most dramatic and useful modes of creative problem solving is hunch or intuition. There was a time when intuition was regarded not only as the key to creativity, but as a special mental disposition—a direct pipeline to the essence of things.

Although intuition's role in creativity and innovation appears to be indispensable, it is frequently distrusted and discounted. Distrust of intuition is frequently implied in such phrases as "It was only a hunch," "I'm not going to play any hunches," "It's an ill-defined gut-feeling," or "It's just a woman's intuition." For example, consider the following witticisms: "Intuition: the strange instinct that tells a woman she is right, whether she is or not." (Oscar Wilde); "Women's intuition is the result of millions of years of not thinking." (Rupert Hughes)

This bias is regrettable, for many individuals of great note depended strongly on intuition for their creative breakthroughs. Thomas Alva Edison, for example, had the remarkable ability to generate useful hunches which, when tested, turned out to be right. He learned to completely trust the feeling of certainty accompanying his intuitions. Similarly, Albert Einstein said, "I believe in intuition and inspiration. . . . At times I feel certain while not knowing the reason. The really valuable method of thought to arrive at a logically coherent system is intuitition."[1] In much of his work, Einstein did not take the slow, painful, step-by-step process to solution, but relied, instead, on "feeling" his way to the right solution. Carson Jeffries, a prominent contemporary physicist at the University of California, Berkeley, remarks on his own intuitive process in the following way: "All of the good ideas (that is, sudden insight into the understanding of a phenomenon I have experimentally discovered, or the mental invention of a new experimental method) I have had in physics came like this: I would be absorbed in the analysis of a problem and excited by a glimpse of a solution, but could not really see the solution, only the expectancy. At some other time, often while going to sleep or waking up, I would get a really good idea—so good that I would get up and jot down a few notes (sometimes symbols). Then I would write out the full idea the next day in my idea journal. Even while mostly asleep I was quite aware that it was a really good idea because it excited me and made me happy. In the awake state, when I see something clearly (something I have been trying fruitlessly to understand), I suddenly feel really good—a warm, sensual body pleasure. I think I also feel this while sleeping and this is what wakes me up."[2]

## SOME SUCCESS STORIES

As a mental shortcut, intuition has been responsible for the dramatic success stories of many prominent inventors and businesspeople. The history of technology and innovation clearly shows that the ideas that gave rise to successful new inventions and products came as a result of intuitive perceptions that were only later tested and verified. One classic case of an uncanny ability to know what would happen next is that of Edwin H. Land, president of Polaroid Corporation and inventor of the Polaroid camera. His original invention met with stiff resistance from his associates. Extensive market research indicated that there would be little or no demand for the camera: It would be too expensive to be sold as a toy and not up to the standards demanded of a fine camera. Fortunately, Land's intuition prevailed and he became the central figure in one of the all-time success stories in business.

Another prominent industrialist who sustained a hunch with great courage is George I. Long, then president of Ampex Corporation. Right after the war, when the television boom started, Long guessed that a product permitting the transcriptions of TV programs for distribution and rebroadcast would tap a huge potential market. Several other firms had considered the idea and had conducted preliminary research. But they all felt that the technical difficulties were too great, and they were dubious about the potential market value of the product. Ampex at the time considered itself too small to tackle the problem, but so strong was George Long's hunch about the success of such a product that the company risked the costly development project. The decision was fortunate; the hunch paid off. The result was videotape, which established Ampex as a leader in the industry.

More and more evidence is now accumulating that the success for entrepreneurs and executives, who frequently have to make firm decisions on the basis of incomplete information and data, depends to a large extent on their willingness and capacity for intuitive decision making. It is their intuitive ability to arrive at effective decisions together with a courage to take risks that determines the success of their organizations. The courage to take risks should be emphasized because so many executives fail not because of any dearth of good hunches, but because of not having the guts to implement them.

## INTUITION AND PROFITS

John Mihalasky of the Newark College of Engineering and his associates have lately been testing hundreds of business executives for intuitive ability, and they are convinced that effective, superior decision making correlates highly with intuitive ability.[3]

For one of their experiments they chose 25 executives who had held top decision-making jobs for five years in their respective companies. All came from small manufacturing companies (less than $50 million in sales) to make sure that decision making was not "contaminated" or diffused by committees.

The results were highly significant. Of the 25 men selected, 12 had doubled their companies' profits in five years, and 11 of those 12 scored way above the chance level on the intuition test.

One man who had scored highest on the test had increased his company's annual profit from $1.3 million to $19.4 million. Conversely, of the 13 men who had not doubled profits, 7 scored below the chance level, 1 at the chance level, and 5 above it. Those 5, however, had each increased profits 50 percent to 100 percent—close to the doubling goal.

## SUSPICION OF INTUITION

Psychologists have discovered of late that many individuals are suspicious of intuition at the peril of inhibiting their creative capacities. Thus Jerome S. Bruner of Harvard University says: "Intuitive thinking, the training of hunches, is a much-neglected and essential feature of productive thinking, not only in formal academic disciplines but also in *everyday* life. The shrewd guess, the fertile hypothesis, the courageous leap to a tentative conclusion—these are the most valuable coin of the thinker at work, whatever his line of work."[4] Similarly, Mason Haire of the University of California, a consulting psychologist to many industrial firms, says: "It is practically impossible to be truly creative without intuitive leaps."[5] And Itzhak Bentov, contemporary scientist and inventor, describes the brain as a hologram, and asserts that it is basically on the intuitive level that creative activity takes place. He believes that creative people rely heavily on intuition, and says: "Intuition is a way of knowing without getting there in the linear, rational way we normally function."[6]

## WHAT THE SAGES SAY

Many of the world's most respected thinkers have acknowledged that intuitive thinking underlines all logical thought, as it does all creative problem solving. Following is a sample of statements made by many of them:

Intuitive knowledge rates above empirical knowledge.

*Spinoza*

Knowledge has three degrees—opinion, science, and illumination. The means or instrument of the first is sense; of the second, dialectic; of the third, intuition. This last is absolute knowledge founded on the identity of the mind knowing with the object known.

*Plotinus*

Reason at its height cannot attain complete grasp and a self-contained assurance. It must fall back upon intuition.

*John Dewey*

The healthy understanding is not the logical, argumentative, but the intuitive.

*Thomas Carlyle*

In the complicated situations of life, we have to solve numerous problems and make many decisions. It is absurd to think that reason should be our guide in all cases. Reason is too slow and too difficult. We do not have the necessary data or we cannot simplify our problems sufficiently to apply the methods of reasoning. What then must we do? Why not do what the human race has always done—use the abilities we have, our common sense, judgment and experience. We underrate the importance of intuition.

*Irving Langmuir*
Nobel prize winner

Intuition for the writer is what experiment is for the learned, with the difference that in the case of the learned the work of the intelligence precedes and in the case of the writer it follows.

*Marcel Proust*

Intuition is the foundation of all processes of reasoning; it illuminates their birth, it directs their development. It is a lighthouse at the starting point, lighting up the ocean of science; it traces, by means of its rays projected into the distance, a golden track which the logician has to follow to arrive at the port of his conclusion. Intuition and reasoning interpenetrate; intuition makes the beginning, deduction carries on the work, but they are always in collaboration.

*Bernard Bosanquet*
philosopher

It is this force of intuition, permitting a man to think his way vitally into the true current of life-unfolding instead of analyzing it fallaciously in terms of static word symbols, that allows intelligence to correct those bad habits which are so paralyzing to creative speculation.

*Richard Guggenheimer*
philosopher

It is exactly this source of creative intuition which should interest us—that quality which so clearly distinguishes the great man of business from the mere money-maker, the statesman from the politician, the truly rational man from the mere dialectitian, the scholar from the recorder and the artist from the reproducer. Strange though it sounds, if our colleges and universities forget this intuitive center of the human mind, their instruction, however accurate and diligent, may bury creativeness.

*Robert Ulich*
philosopher

By intuition is meant the kind of intellectual sympathy by which one places oneself within an object in order to coincide with what is unique in it and consequently inexpressible.

*Henry Bergson*

Strictly speaking, there is hardly any completely logical discovery. Some intervention of intuition issuing from the unconscious is necessary at least to initiate the logical work.

*Jacques Hadamaard*
mathematician

A psychology of perception which neglects the intuitive matrix is a psychology of surfaces, not of solids.

*Gardner Murphy*
psychologist

Learning to tune in to your intuitive flashes is an integral part of getting in touch with more of the possibilities that exist for you, regardless of what your occupation or your interests may be.

*Frances E. Vaughan*
psychologist

Intuition is the basic process of all understanding.

*Susan Langer*
philosopher

Only intuition gives true psychological understanding both of oneself and others. . . . As a normal function of the human psyche, it can be activated simply by eliminating the various obstacles to its unfolding.

*Roberto Assagioli*
psychologist

It is intuitive reason that grasps the first principles.

*Aristotle*

Intuition is the basic foundation of the beautiful, of moral norms, and of religious values. It has furnished the initial impulse to an enormous number of sensory and dialectic discoveries in all fields of human knowledge and values.

*Pitirim Sorokin*
philosopher

The greatest insight, thought and art concerning the human condition and its divine aspirations are rooted in the phenomenon of inner vision.

*Jose* and *Miriam Arguelles*

## WHAT IS INTUITION?

Although any single definition of intuitive thinking is almost certain to be partial and incomprehensive, the process can be defined "operationally." It is an experiential, holistic way of knowing or reasoning where the weighing and balancing of evidence are carried on unconsciously. Intuitive perceptions and "knowings" invariably ring true, even though we often do not know *how* we know what we know. The word *intuition* comes from the Latin *in-tueri,* which roughly means looking, regarding, or knowing from within.

Mason Haire, for example, defines intuition as a case of the mind's performing rapidly, below the level of conscious awareness, the intermediate steps of induction and deduction which are performed consciously, but much more slowly, in analytic thought.[7]

Intuition sometimes appears in awareness only as a vague feeling or hunch, but if focused on and attended to, it can develop into an increasingly clear and useful perception. Intuition can provide very specific and concrete solutions to problems, yet the person even with vivid perceptions retains the quality of knowing without knowing how he or she knows.

## INTUITIVE VERSUS ANALYTICAL MODES

Further clarification can be obtained by comparing intuitive thinking to the analytical mode of thinking. Jerome S. Bruner compares the two this way: "Analytic thinking characteristically proceeds a step at a time. Steps are explicit and usually can be adequately reported by the thinker to another individual. Such thinking proceeds with relatively full awareness of the information and operations involved. It may involve careful and deductive reasoning, often using mathematics or logic and an explicit plan of attack. Or it may involve a step-by-step process of induction and experiment, utilizing principles of research design and statistical analysis.

"Intuitive thinking usually does not advance in careful, well-defined steps. Indeed, it tends to involve maneuvers based seemingly on an implicit perception of the total problem. The thinker arrives at an answer, which may be right or wrong, with little if any awareness of the process by which he reached it. He rarely can provide an adequate account of how he obtained his answer, and he may be unaware of just what aspects of the problem situation he was responding to.

"Usually, intuitive thinking rests on familiarity with the domain of knowledge involved and with its structure, which makes it possible for the thinker to leap about, skipping steps and employing short cuts in a manner that requires a later rechecking of conclusions by more analytic means, whether deductive or inductive."[8]

George Turin of the University of California, Berkeley, states that the following elements are involved in an intuitive approach:

- The ability to know how to attack a problem without being sure *how* you know.
- The ability to relate a problem in one field to seemingly different problems in other fields.
- The ability to recognize what is peripheral and what is central, without having understood the problem fully.
- The ability to know in advance the general nature of the solution.
- The ability to recognize when a solution *must* be right, first because "it feels right."[9]

## INTUITION AND CREATIVITY

Is there any experimental evidence that a high correlation exist between intuitive ability and creativity? In an extensive study, Donald W. MacKinnon and his associates at the University of California tested hundreds of creative and noncreative subjects in a number of fields. One of the tests used was the Myers-Briggs Type Indicator, which distinguishes between two cognitive orientations: a preference for sense-perception (sensation) versus a preference for intuitive-perception (intuition). The individual who favors sense-perception is "inclined to focus upon his immediate sensory experience." The individual concentrates on the sensory attributes of his experience and centers his attention on existing facts as they are given. In contrast, the intuitive-perceptive person "immediately and instinctively perceives the deeper meanings and possibilities inherent in situations and ideas which he experiences." He is "ever alert to links and bridges between what is present and that which is not yet thought of." The person focuses habitually upon what may be, rather than upon what is.[10]

On the test, over 90 percent of the creative subjects showed a marked preference for intuition. In the case of the less creative or noncreative individuals, the percentage preference for intuition was considerably lower. MacKinnon concludes: "It is not that this finding is surprising. One would not expect creative persons to be stimulus-and-object bound, but instead, ever alert to the as-yet-not realized. It is rather the *magnitude* of the preference for intuitive perception that is so striking among highly creative persons."[11]

The psychologist Malcolm Westcott offers the following profile of those individuals who habitually use the intuitive mode in their problem-solving apporaches: "They tend to be unconventional and comfortable in their unconventionality. They are confident and self-sufficient, and do not base their identities on membership in social groups. . . . Their investments appear to be primarily in abstract issues . . . [and] they explore uncertainties and entertain doubts far more than the other groups do, and they live with these doubts and uncertainties without fear. They enjoy taking risks, and are willing to expose themselves to criticism and challenge. . . . They describe themselves as independent, foresighted, confident, and spontaneous."[12]


## THE RIGHT/LEFT HEMISPHERES


Perhaps the strongest support for the value and validity of intuitive thinking comes from recent scientific research which shows that the two hemispheres of the human brain mediate and process different kinds of information and handle different kinds of tasks and problems. The left hemisphere (in Western culture, the more dominant and "overdeveloped") specializes in verbal and numerical information processed sequentially in a linear fashion. The left hemisphere is the active, verbal, logical, rational, and analytic part of the brain. The right hemisphere is the intuitive, experimental, nonverbal part of the brain, and it deals in images and holistic, relational grasping of complex configurations and structures. It creates metaphors, analogies, and new combinations of ideas. (See Table 3 for comparison of the left/right hemisphere functions and modes.)

**Table 3**   COMPARISON OF LEFT/RIGHT HEMISPHERE FUNCTIONS

| Left Mode | Right Mode |
|---|---|
| LOGICAL, ANALYTICAL, SEQUENTIAL, LINEAR: drawing conclusions based on logical order of things; figuring things out in a sequential order, step by step, part by part, one element after another, in an ordered way; proceeding in terms of linked thoughts, one idea directly following another, leading to a convergent conclusion; going from premises to conclusions in a series of orderly, logical steps. Utilizing precise, exact connotations: right/wrong, yes/no, and so forth. | INTUITIVE, HOLISTIC, GESTALT, NONLINEAR: utilizing intuitive feeling of how things fit, belong, or go together; making leaps of insight based on hunches, feelings, incomplete data, patterns, and imagery; perceiving through pattern recognition and spacial references where things are in relation to other things, and how parts connect to form wholes; holographic perception and recognition of gestalts, overall patterns, structures, configurations, complex relationships all at once, simultaneously; multiple processing of information, arriving at conclusions without proceeding through logical, intermediary steps. Recognition of complex figures and abstract patterns. |
| CONVERGENT THINKING: one conclusion or alternative; one meaning. | DIVERGENT THINKING: many conclusions or alternatives; many meanings. |
| RATIONAL: basing conclusions on facts and reason. | NONRATIONAL: does not require basis of reason or facts. |
| CONSCIOUS PROCESSING | SUBCONSCIOUS or PRECONSCIOUS PROCESSING |
| LITERAL MEANING | METAPHORICAL / ANALOGICAL MEANING: perceiving likenesses between disparate things, grasping of metaphorical likenesses. |
| VERBAL, SEMANTIC: language, speech, counting, naming, reading. | NONVERBAL: use of imagery. |
| ABSTRACT: selectively separating a small part or subsystem and having it represent the whole. | CONCRETE: relating to things or whole systems as they are, in the here-and-now. |
| CAUSAL | ACAUSAL |
| EXPLICIT | TACIT |
| CONTROLLED, CONSISTENT | EMOTIVE, AFFECT-LADEN |
| REALISTIC THINKING: strong reality orientation. | FANTASY, REVERIE, DAYDREAMING |
| DOMINANT (usually) | NONDOMINANT: quiet |
| INTELLECTUAL, FORMAL | SENSUOUS, EXPERIENTIAL |

**Table 3** (continued)

| Left Mode | Right Mode |
| --- | --- |
| SHARP FOCAL AWARENESS | DIFFUSE AWARENESS |
| ACTIVE | RECEPTIVE |
| LINEAR TIME: keeping track of time, sequencing one thing after another. | TIMELESSNESS NONTEMPORAL: without sense of time. |
| MATHEMATICAL, SCIENTIFIC | ARTISTIC, MUSICAL, SYMBOLIC |
| DIRECTED | FREE, ASSOCIATIONAL, TOLERANT of AMBIGUITY |
| PROPOSITIONAL | IMAGINATIVE |
| OBJECTIVE | SUBJECTIVE |
| PUBLIC KNOWLEDGE | PRIVATE, IDIOSYNCRATIC KNOWLEDGE |
| JUDGMENTAL, EVALUATIVE | NONJUDGMENTAL, NONCRITICAL: willing to suspend judgment |

## HOW TO USE INTUITIVE THINKING

Some people are better at tuning into and using intuitive approaches than are others. From individuals successful in their reliance on intuitive thinking, these general rules for when and how to rely on it can be offered.

### Watch for Bias

Do not confuse intuitive thinking with intimately personal, subjective thinking. It often emerges as a result of prejudices, biases, fear, wishful thinking, or purely emotional reactions. It takes constant analysis of one's thinking to be able to separate genuine intuitive grain from emotional chaff. Some intuitive feelings and insights can be confused with wishful thinking or anxiety. With some individuals self-deception remains a formidable obstacle to genuine intuitive insights. If an apparently genuine intuitive perception or insight turns out to be dead wrong, it did not emerge from intuition, but from self-deception or from wishful or fearful thinking.

## Keep a Record

First determine how strong your intuitive ability is. Keep a record in a diary or journal of the intuitive insights or hunches that have occurred. Rate them objectively. If a majority or a reasonable number of them have worked out, then cultivate and pay attention to your intuitions. Diary-keeping is the best way to check whether you have genuine intuitive hunches or mainly wishful projections. If, after follow-up, you discover that many of your hunches turn out to be inaccurate, take stock and try to learn how your personal interests, wishes, fears, and anxieties tend to distort your perceptions and block the way to clear and valid intuitions.

## Realize It Is a Normal Function

Realize that intuitive thinking is a perfectly normal function of the brain. It is probably not related to clairvoyance, mystical precognition, or similar phenomena.

Intuitive thinking requires thorough spadework on a problem. It requires getting basic facts and information before intuitive processes can take over. Thus Jerome Bruner says, "Individuals who have extensive familiarity with a subject matter appear more often to leap intuitively into a decision or to a solution of a problem—one which later proves to be appropriate."[13]

## Use a Combined Approach

Use intuitive and analytic modes of thought in combination. Depending on the problem, either one or the other mode should be predominant. Where the intuitive mode is used first, the analytic mode should be tried afterward. Actually, all intuitive thinking should be transposed into linear, logical order for articulation and implementation. Truly effective problem solvers are the ones who couple the right brain processes with those of the left.

## COMPLEX PROBLEMS

Intuition is used to its greatest advantage in solving problems that involve many complex, interrelated factors, as most problems do. When you have many variables, logical reasoning or quantitative techniques are frequently inadequate for synthesizing all the elements into a coherent whole. The intuitive process, by comparison, is manifold. Its multiple processing of information enables it to carry out a work of synthesis.

In some problem situations, failure to reach a good solution is due to inability to view the problem in proper perspective. One may, for example, be so concerned with certain facets of the problem that he or she fails to see others containing the element of a better solution. Cultivated intuitive ability also enables one to recognize the possibilities inherent in many complex situations. One reason for this is the ability of intuition to delve into the vast storehouse of knowledge in the subconscious, where everything is stored that one has learned and experienced both consciously and subliminally. Tapping into this rich storehouse enables one to perceive or sense the potential, though as yet not realized, possibilities inherent in many complex situations or problems.

There may be connections and segregations in a problem that often stay out of the clutches of one's concretizing and conceptualizing mind, that are beyond one's analytical powers, but that may be "divined" through intuition. Similarly, in many business and personal problems, most of the parameters and variables involved to not exist in a quantitative form. In such cases, the person should have the courage to arrive at an intuitive viewpoint. In one recent study by the psychologist D.K. Simonton, in which creativity and problem complexity were related to intuitive versus analytical problem solving, it was found that the relative effectiveness of each mode definitely depends on the nature of the problem. The more creative subjects, in particular, found the intuitive mode more effective for complex tasks and analysis more effective for simple tasks.[14]

The intuitive mode is not opposed to the rational, cognitive mode, but works with it in a complementary fashion. Typically, intuitive insights both precede and follow in a cyclical, oscillating way the exhaustive use of analysis, reason, and logic. The physicist Fritjof Capra says: "Rational knowledge and rational activities certainly constitute the major part of scientific research, but are not all there is to it. The rational part of research would, in fact, be useless if it were not complemented by the intuition that gives scientists new insights and makes them creative. These insights tend to come suddenly, and characteristically not when sitting at a desk working out the equations, but when relaxing, in the bath, during a walk in the woods, on the beach, etc. During these periods of relaxation after concentrated intellectual activity, the intuitive mind seems to take over and can produce the sudden clarifying insights which give so much joy and delight to scientific research."[15]

## ANALYZE AND WAIT

Genuine intuitive insights are not under the conscious control of the will. One cannot predict when they will come. One must tackle problems consciously, and learn as much about them as possible, using the analytic processes. All known data must be acquired (laziness usually produces faulty hunches). The intuitive hunch may come in a flash while tackling the problem, or later when the problem is put aside. The common expression "sleep on it" refers to allowing the intuitive-incubative processes to take over problem solving. Many creative people report finding solutions to apparently intractable problems either in the morning upon awakening or during reverie. Dr. Jonas Salk, after tedious, long, drawn-out experiments seeking ways to immunize against polio, Salk made one morning, upon awakening, an intuitive leap to the correct vaccine. He stated: "It is always with excitement that I wake up in the morning wondering what my intuition will toss up to me, like gifts from the sea. I work with it, and rely upon it. It's my partner."[16]

The important thing is to recognize the value of the intuitive hunch when it occurs. Don't brush it aside or dismiss it as something irrational or unnatural. R. Buckminster Fuller, creator of the geodesic dome, called intuition "cosmic fishing." He said, "You feel a nibble, then you've got to hook the fish. Too many people get a hunch, then light up a cigarette and forget about it."[17] Use and act upon your intuitions, for they can be the springboard for successfully attaining your desired goals in life.

Frances E. Vaughan, a psychologist on the faculty of the California Institute of Transpersonal Psychology, offers these valuable guidelines for awakening intuition, not only for problem solving, but for expanding your capacity for perceiving, understanding, and knowing more:

> *Intention*—The first requirement for consciously awakening intuition is a clear intention to do so. Intuition is already within you, but to awaken it you have to value it and *intend* to develop it.

*Time*—Your willingness to devote time to tuning in to your intuition, making a space for its unfolding in your life, is part of valuing and developing it.

*Relaxation*—Letting go of physical and emotional tension gives intuition the space to enter your conscious awareness.

*Silence*—Intuition flourishes in silence. Learning to quiet the mind is therefore part of the training for awakening intuition. Various meditative practices are useful in learning to maintain the necessary inner silence.

*Honesty*—Willingness to face self-deception and to be honest with yourself and others is essential. Creating any kind of smokescreen interferes with clear vision. Giving up pretenses is a big step in awakening intuition.

*Receptivity*—Learning to be quiet and receptive allows intuition to unfold. Too much activity or conscious programming gets in the way of intuitive awareness that emerges when a receptive attitude is cultivated.

*Sensitivity*—Finely tuned sensitivity to both inner and outer processes provides more information and expands intuitive knowing. Sensitivity to energy awareness and the quality of experience is particularly useful.

*Nonverbal Play*—Drawing, music, movement, clay and other forms of nonverbal expression done in a spirit of play, rather than for the purpose of goal-oriented achievement, provide excellent channels for activating intuitive, right-hemisphere functions.

*Trust*—Trusting the process, trusting yourself, trusting your experience are the keys to trusting and developing your intuition.

*Openness*—If you are afraid of being seen, you may close up and then be unable to see. Being open to all experiences, both inner and outer, gives intuition the space it needs to develop fully.

*Courage*—Fear gets in the way of direct experience and often generates deception. Your willingness to experience and confront your fears will facilitate the expansion of intuition.

*Acceptance*—A nonjudgmental attitude, an acceptance of things as they are, including self-acceptance, allows intuition to function freely.

*Nonattachment*—The willingness to let things be as they are, rather than trying to make them be the way you would like them to be, or the way you think they should be, allows intuition to emerge. You can see things as they are only when desires and fears are out of the way.

*Daily Practice*—Intuitive awareness grows with daily attention. If you discount or neglect it most of the time and only want it to perform occasionally, it may not respond.

*Journal Keeping*—Keeping a record of intuitive flashes, hunches, insights and images that come to mind spontaneously at any time of the day or night, can help stabilize them.

*Support Group*—Finding one, two, or more friends with whom you can share your interest in the development of intuition, as well as your successes, failures, hopes, and fears, can facilitate and accelerate the process of development. Sharing experience with someone who is willing to listen without judging or interpreting, is very useful.

*Enjoyment*—Following intuition does not always feel good. At times it may seem difficult and entail arduous work. At other times it may be effortless. Enjoying the creative resources of intuition is based on the intrinsic satisfaction of expanding consciousness, taking responsibility for your life, and surrendering to your own true nature.[18]

# REFERENCES

[1] A. Moszkowski, *Conversations with Einstein*, trans. Henry L. Brose (New York: Horizon Press, 1970), p. 96.

[2] Frances E. Vaughan, *Awakening Intuition.* (New York: Anchor Books, 1979), p. 151.

[3] Eugene Raudsepp, "Intuition: A Neglected Decision-Making Tool," *Machine Design,* September 25, 1980, pp. 91–92.

[4] Eugene Raudsepp, "Can Hunches Be Trusted?" *Chemical Engineering,* November 19, 1979, p. 168.

[5] Eugene Raudsepp, "Learn to Play Your Hunches," *Machine Design,* April 15, 1965, p. 134.

[6] Vaughan, *Awakening Intuition,* p. 171.

[7] Raudsepp, "Learn to Play," p. 135.

[8] Eugene Raudsepp, "Can You Trust Your Hunches?" *Management Review,* April 1960, p. 6.

[9] Raudsepp, "Can Hunches?" p. 168.

[10] Ibid.

[11] Ibid., p. 170.

[12] Malcolm Westcott, *Toward a Contemporary Psychology of Intuition.* (New York: Holt, Rinehart & Winston, 1968), p. 121.

[13] Raudsepp, "Can Hunches?" p. 170.

[14] D.K. Simonton, "Creativity, Task Complexity, and Intuitive versus Analytical Problem Solving," *Psychological Reports,* 1975, pp. 351–54.

[15] Fritjof Capra, *The Tao of Physics.* (Berkeley, Ca.: Shambala, 1975), p. 31.

[16] Ray Rowan, "Those Business Hunches Are More Than Blind Faith," *Fortune,* April 23, 1979, p. 88.

[17] Ibid.

[18] Frances E. Vaughan, *Awakening Intuition.* (New York: Anchor Books, 1979), p. 228.

# 7

# FANTASIZING
# AND CREATIVITY

Until recently, daydreaming, or fantasizing, was considered either a waste of time or a symptom of maladjustment. Most psychologists branded habitual daydreaming as evidence of neurotic tendencies or as an escape from the stern responsibilities of the workaday world. They warned that habitual daydreaming would eventually alienate a person from society and reduce his or her effectiveness in coping with problems in real life. Even those behavioral scientists who were more indulgent, considered daydreaming a childish or adolescent habit, causing students to get bad grades and adults to fail at their jobs. Even at its best, daydreaming was considered "a sublimated drive gratification" or a "compensatory substitute" for the real things in life. The most prevalent stereotype of a daydreamer pictures him or her to be a person lost in fantasies, busily weaving images of either heroic Walter Mitty–type achievements, travel to distant never-never-lands, or romantic conquests and sexual fulfillment.

Marvin Rosenberg of the University of California, Berkeley,

gives a good description of our prevailing attitudes toward daydreaming. "For most ordinary persons past infancy, a daydream is often categorized as a secret vice, so embarrassing in its persistence that it can be admitted only as a guilty indulgence. One of the first things children learn from well-intentioned parents is to apply themselves to reality, not to dream. Parents and teachers know too well what daydreams are like: cottony visions of glory, or, even worse, exercises in lust or aggression. (Where else *can* children usually exercise lust or aggression in a socially approved way, except in fantasy?)"[1]

As with anything carried to excess, daydreaming can be harmful. There are those who substitute a fantasy life for the rewards of activity in the real world. And, when the fantasy addict withdraws from people, when he or she can no longer cope with reality, psychological health is impaired.

But these situations are very rare, indeed. The truth is that most people suffer from a *lack* of daydreaming, rather than an *excess* of it. We now know how valuable daydreaming really is. There is a growing realization that if we were completely prevented from daydreaming, our emotional balance would be rendered precarious. Not only would we be less able to deal with pressures of day-to-day existence, but our self-direction and control over our lives would be in danger of being relinquished.

## THE DREAM REVOLUTION

Attitudes toward daydreaming have been, in a sense, much like the attitudes toward dreaming in our sleep. There was a time when dreaming was thought to interfere with normal sleep and rob us of the necessary rest it is meant to provide. Recent experiments on dreaming, however, indicate that not only are dreams a normal part of the process of sleep, but that a certain amount of dreaming each night is vital to mental health.

Dr. William Dement, who conducted extensive experiments on the significance of dreaming at Mount Sinai Hospital in New York, reports that those subjects whose dreams were interrupted regularly, exhibited such emotional disturbances as hypertension, anxiety, irritability, and difficulty in concentrating. "One of the subjects,"

Dr. Dement reported, "quit the study in apparent panic, and two insisted on stopping, presumably because the stress was too great."[2] It was also observed that in five subjects there was a considerable increase in appetite during the period of "dream-deprivation." As soon as the subjects were allowed to dream again, all psychological disturbances vanished.

More drastic experiments in Edinburgh, Scotland, have supported these findings. Volunteers who kept awake as long as 108 hours at a stretch, when finally permitted to sleep, dreamed considerably more than usual. "It is as though a pressure to dream builds up with the accruing dream deficit during successive dream-deprivation nights," says Dr. Dement, and adds that "if dream suppression was carried on long enough, the result would be a serious disruption of the personality."[3]

## DAYDREAMING IS A SAFETY VALVE

In a similar fashion, prolonged daydream deprivation results in mounting anxiety and tension. Finally, many people find that the need can no longer be suppressed, and daydreaming erupts spontaneously.

During times of stress, our nervous system erects, by means of daydreaming, a temporary shelter to shield us from the "icy winds" of reality, much in the same way that a house protects our bodies from the elements. Both may be seen as forms of "escapism," but no sane man or woman wants to spend his or her life in an unrelieved battle for survival. Surely we are entitled to occasional "strategic withdrawals" to recoup our forces.

## SOME RECENT FINDINGS

Recent research on daydreaming indicates that it is an intrinsic part of daily life and that a certain amount of daydreaming each day is essential for relaxation.

But the beneficial effects of daydreaming go beyond relaxation and the reduction of tension. According to experiments conducted by Joan T. Freyberg, a New York City based psychotherapist, day-dreaming significantly helps learning ability, powers of concentration, attention span, and the ability to interact and communicate with others. She also discovered that those of her patients who easily engage in daydreaming, usually respond more quickly to treatment and are better able to cope with life's frustrations and crises.

In another experiment with school children, she observed that daydreaming improved their concentration. "There was less running around, more happy feelings, more talking and playing with each other, and more attention to detail," Freyberg reports.[4] It has also been found that those children who daydream regularly are least likely to develop crippling emotional disorders.

In still another experiment, the psychologist Sara Similansky discovered that the individuals who were taught how to daydream, significantly improved their language and other skills. And Jerome L. Singer at Yale University found that daydreaming resulted in improved self-control and enhanced creative thinking.[5] Singer also pointed out that daydreaming is a way to creatively improve upon reality, and that it helps a person to cope with delay, frustration, and deprivation. It frequently helps us to change difficult situations into more manageable ones, and it gives impetus to meaningful future planning. Daydreaming gives us greater strength and resolve to overcome the obstacles and difficulties as we move toward our objectives; it is a powerful spur to achievement.

Other clinical and experimental research has indicated that day-dreaming helps us to better understand our own behavior and to achieve a more intimate rapport with, and acceptance of, our inner feelings. This, in turn, helps us to relate better to other people in our environment.

Attitudes toward daydreaming have changed considerably in a relatively short time span; from considering daydreaming as a trivial or pathological self-absorption, to the present view that it is an important human skill for the creative enrichment of life, available to anyone who wants to practice it.

## SEND YOUR MIND ON VACATION

Daydreaming not only provides us psychological protection from worries, frustrations, and stresses, it is also, as previously noted, an effective relaxation technique. By inducing relaxation, daydreaming effectively removes tension, overagitated feelings, anxiety, and worry, and restores the necessary flow of strength and equilibrium. As the surgeon and author Maxwell Maltz puts it: "It depressurizes you from tensions, worry, pleasure, stresses and strains. It refreshes you and enables you to return to your workaday world better prepared to cope with it."[6]

A prominent executive of an electronics firm who makes it a habit to daydream a few minutes every day claims that it adds considerably to his creative energy. It restores that flow of strength that enables him to return refreshed to a difficult task. He reports that after a brief respite of daydreaming he feels more vigorous and zestful, and that he is able to handle sudden pressures and crisis situations more efficiently.

Other individuals have reported that daydreaming helps them to recall many tasks, obligations, and objectives that they had forgotten in the press of practical daily concerns.

Workers who are tied to the frustrations and monotony of routine tasks have reported that daydreaming helps them to keep interested in their work for longer periods of time and that it reduces the discomfort of monotony and frustration.

Many other people who enjoy the pleasure and excitement of daydreaming report how it refreshes their minds and buoys their spirits. Dorothea Brande, the famous author, says that daydreaming always gives her a tremendous surge of vitality: "It seems as though my mind gave a great sigh of relief at the liberation and stretched itself to its fullest extent."[7]

Other people who daydream regularly have reported that they emerge from the "vacation"—the change of pace or scenery that daydreaming provides—not only more relaxed and refreshed, but also more optimistic, exhilarated, enthusiastic, and purposeful. Some even claim that they experience a feeling of "lightness" in their bodies. Perceptions and senses, too, are sharpened: Colors seem brighter, more intense, and objects seem to take on greater depth.

As these reports show, the beneficial aspects of daydreaming can act to restore your feeling of mental and physical wellbeing. While it siphons off the harmful and painful feelings of tension and frustration, it builds up a reservoir of creative energy. In this sense, the habit of daydreaming is almost like opening a special "energy bank account" into which you deposit for the purpose of having resources available during periods of crisis or emergency.

## DAYDREAMING CAN SOLVE YOUR PROBLEMS

The value of daydreaming, however, does not stop with the benefits already mentioned. It has been found that it also improves a person's ability to be better attuned to practical, immediate concerns; to solve everyday problems creatively; to make decisions; and to come up with new ideas more readily. Contrary to popular belief, incessant and conscious effort at solving a problem is in reality one of the most inefficient ways of tackling it. Although initial effort is necessary when we face a problem, it has been discovered that an effective solution to an especially difficult or bothersome problem frequently occurs when conscious attempts to solve it have been suspended. Answers to intractable problems, which seem to come from "out of the blue," invariably arise from daydreaming about your problem in a relaxed way. This is because daydreaming enables you to break out of the tyranny of your intellect into the freedom of your intuition. Inability to relax, to let go of a conscious preoccupation with a problem and daydream, often prevents solving it.

## DAYDREAMING AND THE WORLD'S GREATEST INVENTIONS

Many famous scientists and inventors have taken full advantage of the relaxed moments of daydreaming. Their biographies reveal that the best ideas occurred to them when they were relaxing and daydreaming. It is well known, for example, that Sir Isaac Newton solved many of his most difficult problems when his attention was waylaid by private musings and fantasies. Thomas Alva Edison also knew the value of half-waking states, and whenever confronted with a seemingly insurmountable hitch that defied all his conscious efforts, he would stretch out on his couch in his workshop—brought there for just this purpose—and let fantasies flood his mind.

## GREAT ARTISTS KNOW THE VALUE OF DAYDREAMING

Creative artists, writers, and composers have always drawn heavily upon their inner fantasies and reverie. Johannes Brahms, for example, found that ideas came to him effortlessly only when he approached the state of deep daydreaming. César Franck, the French composer, is said to have walked around with a dream-like gaze in his eyes while he was composing, seemingly totally unaware of his surroundings. John Dewey recognized the importance of reverie in all types of creative work when he stated: "I do not think it can be denied that an element of reverie, of approach to a state of dream, enters into the creation of a work of art, nor that the experience of the work when it is intense often throws one into a similar state. Indeed, it is safe to say that creative conceptions come only to persons who are relaxed to the point of reverie."[8]

But one does not have to be a creative genius to benefit from daydreaming. Growing evidence shows that most people, whatever their occupation and age, can startlingly increase their production of original and creative materials once they learn to daydream. Thus a healthful acceptance and enjoyment of fantasizing can make use of one's inner experiences for both pleasure and creative work. One can experience new creative dimensions in oneself, transcending present limitations.

## DAYDREAMING HELPS IN SELF-DISCOVERY

It has been found that daydreaming does not have to pursue the impossible, the will-o'-the-wisp. On the contrary, for many people a passive retreat into the private world of reverie is their "royal road" to making their reality more meaningful. Daydreaming helps them in self-discovery, in finding out who they are and what they really would want to do. They use daydreaming as a means for self-study, for canvassing alternatives, and for discovering fresh directions, serving as a compass in their future actions. They use it for taking stock of their values, desires, annoyances, wishes, fears, and plans for the future.

Even our best made plans and objectives frequently change or get lost behind the haze and hurry of practical concerns. Daily life, with its constant happenings and changes, tends to modify our situations; and the only way we can retain a leverage on our goals and objectives and pry them loose for examination and reassessment is to retreat back into ourselves to "mull things over." Daydreaming helps us to become more attentive to our inner selves. It helps us to repel as foreign stuff the excess baggage of irrelevant concerns that frequently hinder action on our more fundamental goals. It helps us to put our true concerns, the things that are really relevant to us, into sharper focus. In this way we can actually improve the quality of our lives.

Without periods of daydreaming we run the risk of not investing our lives with goals and values personally and deeply significant to us. And when our goals, needs, and values are inadequately taken account of, our entire life-pattern suffers.

Daydreaming helps us to understand ourselves better and become more authentic and natural. This is important, because individuals with inadequate self-knowledge frequently either attempt to be what they are not or are too ready to conform to the dictates and demands of their immediate environment. With deepened self-knowledge, however, our inherent individuality is allowed to emerge, and we can become more autonomous and self-responsible for our behavior.

## DAYDREAMING AND THE ATTAINMENT OF SUCCESS

Many successful people actually daydream their future successes and achievements. Daydreaming for them bears a direct relationship to its expression in overt behavior.

In sports, for example, John Uelses, former pole-vaulting champion, made use of deliberate, programmed daydreaming. Before each meet he vividly pictured himself clearing the bar at a certain height. He repeatedly visualized not only all the minute details of the act of winning, but actually "saw" the stadium, the crowds present, and even "smelled" the grass and the earth. The resulting memory-traces influenced his actual performance during the meet toward the vividly pictured goal of success.

Jack Nicklaus daydreams before each tournament to attain, what he calls, "the winning feeling." This feeling, as he puts it, "gives me a line to the cup just as clearly as if it's been tatooed on my brain. With that feeling all I have to do is swing the clubs and let nature take its course."[9]

Jim Thorpe, who is considered to be one of the greatest athletes of all time, utilized strong mental imagery to picture success before each sporting event. Author Lew Miller relates this story about him. "Once he was on a ship headed for the Olympics. Other stars were running around the deck or exercising vigorously. The track coach spotted Thorpe, his decathlon entrant, sitting propped against a cabin with his eyes closed. 'What do you think you're doing?' the coach demanded. 'Just practicing,' replied Jim. He then explained that while relaxing he was seeing himself successfully competing in his specialty. History has recorded his legendary feats and record-breaking performances. Jim Thorpe knew instinctively how mental images work."

Lew Miller, who attributes his own almost miraculous recovery from the battle wounds received during World War II to the deliberate evocation of positive mental imagery, states that all of his successful ventures in life were due to vivid daydreaming:

> In every instance, I had pictured that success beforehand. The more vivid the picture and the greater the faith I had in it, the greater the degree of success.
>
> In basketball, I remembered picturing a strong mental image of the ball going through the hoop time after time. When I popped in six or seven long shots in a row it wasn't surprising. I had visualized it happening. I "practiced" seeing myself hitting a softball, driving in runs. When it happened, it was just as if it happened for a second time. I was able to improve my backhand in tennis with "beforehand" mental images. In the same way, I saw myself in reverie, days before a cross-country run finishing in the first ten in a field of 350 top athletes. It happened.
>
> On and on, I recalled the successful incidents in my life and there was always one single common denominator. In each instance I held in mind a strong mental image and clung to it with unbounded faith.[10]

Another person who believed in the practical value of daydreaming was Henry J. Kaiser. He maintained that "you can imagine your future," and believed that a great part of his success in business had been due to the positive use of intense and vivid daydreams. Harry S. Truman claimed that he used daydreaming as a retreat from stresses and strains, for a period of rest and recuperation. "I have a foxhole in my mind," he used to say.

Conrad Hilton visualized operating a hotel in his boyhood, long before he ever acquired one. He said that all his accomplishments were first realized in his imagination during daydreaming.

"Great living starts with a picture, held in some person's imagination, of what he would like some day to do or be. Florence Nightingale dreamed of being a nurse, Edison pictured himself an inventor; all such characters escaped the mere shove or circumstance by imagining a future so vividly that they headed for it." These are the words of the profoundly humanistic thinker Harry Emerson Fosdick, and they show that people can literally daydream themselves to success. Fosdick, aware of the tremendous power of positive daydreaming, offered this advice: "Hold a picture of yourself long and steadily in your mind's eye and you will be drawn toward it. Picture yourself vividly as defeated and that alone will make victory impossible. Picture yourself vividly as winning and that alone will contribute immeasurably to success. Do not picture yourself as anything and you will drift like a derelict."[11]

Several clinics specializing in the treatment of alcoholics make use of the technique of daydreaming to cure alcoholics. Edward McGoldrick, whose Bridge House in New York has a high record of recoveries from alcohol addiction, incorporated daydreaming into his daily treatment modality. Every day his patients are trained and instructed to relax, to close their eyes, and to deliberately picture themselves as sober, responsible, and successful persons, enjoying life to the hilt without the crutch of liquor. After a few weeks of this fantasy-therapy, many patients not only attain sobriety, but a new, more positive and courageous outlook on life.

## VIVID DAYDREAMS IMPROVE SELF-IMAGE

Why would a vivid projection of success help to bring the success about? "Your nervous system cannot tell the difference between an *imagined* experience and a *real* experience," says Maxwell Maltz. "In either case, it reacts automatically to information which you give to it from your forebrain. Your nervous system reacts appropriately to what you think or imagine to be true." He further maintains that the exercise of daydreaming "builds new 'memories' or stored data into your midbrain and central nervous system."[12] These positive memories in turn improve self-image, and improved self-image has a telling impact on a person's behavior and accomplishments.

## HOW TO HARNESS YOUR DAYDREAMS

In order to creatively "engineer" your future, you should picture yourself—as vividly as possible—as you want to be or become, or what you want to have or attain. The important thing to remember is that you have to picture these desired objectives *as if you had already attained them.* Go over the details of these highly pleasant fantasy pictures several times. This procedure will indelibly impress them upon your memory. And these memory traces, or "engrams," as they are also called, will soon start influencing your everyday behavior toward the attainment of the pictured goal of success.

While visualizing this way, you should be alone and completely undisturbed. Close your eyes, for this helps your imagination soar without inhibition. Many people find they obtain better results if they imagine themselves sitting before a large, blank screen onto which they project the picture of their desire. Visual imagery is the predominant modality for daydreaming, and you have to make sure that your imagery is clear and sharp.

Here is a daydream exercise you can do to evoke imagery that shows you what direction your work should take for increased harmony and growth:

Close your eyes. Breathe in and out slowly and deeply. Allow yourself to relax. Go to a level where you can visualize, where images flow freely and easily. Imagine yourself doing work that you enjoy, that makes you feel comfortable. It may be the work you are presently doing or work that is similar—or it may be work that is quite different. Let a series of images flow through your mind—images of different aspects of the work. Notice whether you are working alone or with other people, whether the work is primarily physical or mental. Notice whether you are working outdoors, in a building, or in your home. Are you working for yourself or are you employed by someone? Visualize your work schedule—the hours and days you work, the speed at which you accomplish tasks. Visualize the amount of money you'd like to make, the kind of ego gratification you'd like to get from your work. Be open and alert toward any images that come into your mind.

Visualization gives you a chance to try out work situations without actually doing them in the external world. You can imagine yourself in any job situation you can think of. And you can immediately change any aspect of the job, or visualize an entirely different job. As you do this, you can see how each situation and each change makes you feel. When you experience strong positive feelings such as satisfaction, excitement, and heightened interest, you are touching your pure inner images. When you experience negative feelings such as anxiety, stress, or boredom, you are becoming aware of areas that are far from your vision. You can let these negative images pass, or you can change aspects of the image until it makes you feel good again. If you did not visualize your present work situation in the beginning of this exercise, you can do so now. By paying attention to your feelings and by making changes in the images, you can locate the aspects of your work that bring you the greatest satisfaction. You can also locate the aspects that make you uncomfortable and, through manipulation of the images, discover ways to improve those aspects of your work. When you identify images that make you feel good, hold them in your mind. Using your feelings as a guide, you can evaluate and modify your visualization of your work until it feels intensely right to you, one that is accompanied by strong positive feelings. It is this visualization, that is, program, that you would hold in mind to help you manifest it in the external world.

Some people first mentally relive some successful experience of the past to attain a positive, facilitative mood for daydreaming. When a mood of confidence and optimism has been attained, they then, so to speak, "cloak" it around whatever they want to accomplish or become. Again, the important thing to remember is that the picturing or imagining of desired things must be done as if they were already successfully achieved.

Lew Miller advises that you should build your scenario according to some *immediate* goal you want to attain. "Whatever it is, you write the script as it progresses, projecting yourself actively into as many successful, triumphant scenes as your imagination permits. Concentrate on it with burning desire. Then, turn off the mental imagery and begin to act in daily life as if you already had achieved that goal. Turn on your little theater performance whenever a moment of solitude presents itself. Your faithful portrayal of the role you're playing will cause it to actualize in your life in direct proportion to the belief that you have in your own theatrical production."[13]

While daydreaming, you should be completely free of intrusions from the outer world. Of course, when daydreaming is intense, you will experience a feeling of blissful timelessness, in which the sense of before and after and of things around or outside have completely vanished. Some individuals seem to have the ability to tune into their private selves in the midst of other people. But with most of us, especially when the experience is new, an environment free from outside distraction is necessary. Any sudden distraction or interruption can inhibit the spontaneous flow of images so vital for shaping fantasy. Daydreaming can be best accomplished under conditions in which external stimuli are absent or greatly reduced. Physical isolation from people, in addition to a quiet atmosphere, are mandatory.

A life lived without fantasy and daydream is a seriously impoverished life. Each of us should put aside a few minutes each day and daydream, sort of take a ten or fifteen minute vacation. It is highly beneficial to your physical and mental wellbeing, and you will find that this modest investment in time will add up to a more creative and imaginative, a more satisfied, and a more self-fulfilled you in a relatively short time. The art of successful daydreaming offers a fuller sense of being intensely alive from moment to moment, and this, of course, contributes greatly to the excitement and zest in living.

# REFERENCES

[1] Marvin Rosenberg, "Releasing the Creative Imagination," *Journal of Creative Behavior*, 10 (Third Quarter, 1976), no. 3, 203.

[2] Eugene Raudsepp, "Let Your Mind Wander," *American Way*, October 1979, p. 20.

[3] Ibid.

[4] Eugene Raudsepp, "Let Daydreaming Improve Your Life," *Chemical Engineering*, April 23, 1979, p. 154

[5] Raudsepp, "Let Your Mind," p. 21.

[6] Eugene Raudsepp, "Fantasy Can Make You a Better Manager," *Manage*, July 1979, p. 28.

[7] Eugene Raudsepp, "A New Look at Daydreaming," *Sundancer*, April 1977, p. 53.

[8] John Dewey, *Art as Experience*. (New York: Capricorn Books, 1958), pp. 275–76.

[9] Raudsepp, "A New Look," p. 54.

[10] Raudsepp, "Let Daydreaming," p. 155.

[11] Harry E. Fosdick, *On Being a Real Person*. (New York: Harper & Brothers, 1943), p. 174.

[12] Raudsepp, "Fantasy," p. 29.

[13] Raudsepp, "Let Daydreaming," p. 155.

# 8

# GUIDELINES TO CREATIVITY

For practically all of us there is a considerable gap between our native creative potential and our actual day-to-day performance in solving problems. This gap, however, can be considerably narrowed by the mastery of the creative problem-solving process.

Following are a series of practical guideposts for realizing your maximum brainpower potential and for increasing your creative ability and output in solving problems. Observance and mastery of these principles and procedures will help you to avoid the traps of painful and time-consuming trial and error in the solution of problems and to arrive at a more effective creative method.

Although the specific creative problem-solving procedures of individuals vary considerably, there seems to be an over-all general pattern or procedure which most creative individuals follow. This pattern has been distilled from the study of the procedures used by hundreds of acknowledged creative individuals in a variety of occupations, professions, and fields.

One of the most gratifying things about creative problem solving is that once you have made the beginning, once you have developed a habit of inventively tackling problems, there are almost no limits to the ever-broadening area in which you can use your creative ability.

## THERE MUST BE MOTIVATION

Basic to creative problem solving is a great interest in problems and a strong desire for their solution. For effective creative problem solving, motivation has to be intense.

Those who have tasted the satisfaction of solving problems creatively find such satisfactions adequate to motivate them for further creative effort. On the other hand, those who are inexperienced in creative problem solving need to build up their motivations by building up their self-confidence through a series of smaller successes, before they can tackle more difficult problems. They have to learn to perceive themselves as able to find out things on their own, to do something original and tackle problems in novel ways. This attitude of self-confidence, incidentally, is so important that without it, the requisite feeling of pressure and need to find creative solutions to problems is negligible, if not totally absent. All successful creative individuals have this self-confidence or optimism. They believe that eventually they will get there and achieve success, no matter how many difficulties and failures they initially encounter. This basic optimism keeps them motivated to keep working at and revising their approaches in the face of serious discouragement. Developing this spirit of self-confidence and an optimism that believes that *any* problem can be solved, is already winning more than half of the battle.

## GENERAL BACKGROUND KNOWLEDGE IS VITAL

The individual who has a broad knowledge of many fields and an abundance of accumulated experience can come up with new, significant creative ideas easier and more rapidly than can the individual who has only a detailed, specialized knowledge of only one field. The revelations of creative individuals leave no doubt that thorough immersion in one field has to be coupled with a breadth of experience and knowledge in many other fields. In order to increase the fund of total experience upon which can be built new patterns and configurations when tackling problems, do the following:

• Set time aside to read in fields or areas other than your own particular specialization. This will broaden your perspectives and provide you with new data that may catalyze new ideas. If you are familiar with other points of view and methods, you are in a position to look at your problem from new angles. Sometimes the combining of methods of different fields helps you to obtain an original approach to your problem.

• Start with fields tangential to your area and gradually spread out to areas further removed from your specialty. Always read with the question in mind: "How might I be able to use this?"

• When reading, take notes and keep them—they may be of use months or even years later.

• Collect and file notes, clippings, and ideas that seem useful and original. Keep them organized, available, and, if possible, indexed. Study them occasionally for stimulating your own problem-solving activities.

• Attempt writing or working on a problem outside your own field to increase your familiarity with ideas and sources of reference other than those you need for your immediate area of interest. This will increase your ability to incorporate new information and ideas with your own problem-solving approaches and to facilitate the grouping of ideas into new combinations.

• Engage freely in hobbies that require concentration and mental effort, such as chess, bridge, games, and puzzle-solving. Aside from exercising your problem-solving ability, these types of games are relaxing and help to open your conscious mind to the flashes of insight and ideas lodged in your unconscious. Also engage in handicraft, and in constructing and building hobbies, for these are much more stimulating to creativity than are collecting hobbies.

• Engage in travel, which also serves as a stimulus to creativity for the same reason as hobbies. It relaxes the hold of the conservative orientation of your consciousness, permitting new ideas to emerge from the unconscious.

• Unremittingly and continually exercise your creative powers—this is of paramount necessity. For this reason you should try to approach every problem you encounter as creatively as you can. Observe things around you with the questioning attitude: "How could this be done differently or better?" You should also form the habit of asking yourself questions about as many facets of the problem as you can.

• Pose new questions every day. A questioning, curious, inquiring mind is a creatively active mind. It is also a mind that constantly enlarges the circumference of its awareness. Assume that everything can be improved. Develop heightened sensitivity to problems—an attitude of constructive discontent toward existing and future situations and problems.

• Maintain competence in your chosen field. Information and knowledge obsolescence proceed at an accelerating pace because of the information explosion. Keep abreast of what is happening, but also learn to solve problems and think more creatively. The latter is frequently more important than the mere retention of facts and information. Schedule regular practice sessions for creative problem solving. Develop strong motivation to utilize your creative capacities in problem finding and problem-solving situations.

• Avoid rigid, set patterns of doing things. Overcome fixed ideas and look for new viewpoints; try new ways. Attempt not only for one solution to your problems, but several, and develop the ability to let go of one idea in favor of another. Experiment, and always produce many alternative solutions to your problems.

• Be open and receptive to your own as well as to others' ideas. Recognize that new ideas are fragile, and listen positively to them. Seize on tentative, half-formed ideas and possibilities. A new idea seldom arrives as a completely ready-made package, tied with a red ribbon to be delivered to your boss. Freely entertain and articulate the apparently wild, farfetched, or even silly ideas. Learn to inhibit judgmental thinking when listening to the ideas of others. Being receptive to others will enable you to learn new things. New information is available all around us. Be secure enough to listen to the ideas of others. But most importantly, be secure enough not to be unduly influenced by or concerned about the opinions of others. Refuse to be discouraged by others and persist in spite of obstacles.

• Be alert in observation. Look for similarities, differences, and unique and distinguishing features in objects, situations, products, processes, and ideas. The more new and unusual associations and relationships you can form, the greater your chances of coming up with really creative and original combinations and solutions. Jot down any random thoughts that come to you from time to time.

• Improve your sense of humor and laugh easily. It helps you to put yourself, your problems, and your pressure-jitters into proper perspective. Humor is also an excellent tension-relieving device, and a person is more productively creative when relaxed.

• Adopt a risk-taking attitude. Be willing to fail on occasion. Nothing is more fatal to creativity than the fear of failure. Heed Chester Barnard's sage advice: "To try and fail, is at least to learn. To fail to try is to suffer the inestimable loss of what might have been."[1]

• Have courage and self-confidence. Always proceed on the assumption that you can solve your problems or create the thing you have in your mind's eye. Many people give up just when they are on the brink of solution. Persist and have the tenacity to overcome problems. Be enthusiastic and confident. Goethe once said, "Whatever you can do, or dream you can, begin it. Boldness has genius, power, and magic in it!"

• Learn to know and understand yourself. To improve your creative output, you must deepen your self-knowledge and what you values are. Get to know your real strengths, skills, likes, weaknesses, dislikes, and biases. Accept yourself and be your natural self. The psychologist Clark E. Moustakas states: "Every real individual is a creative person. This intrinsic creativity emerges, or is expressed, when the person is free to use his potentialities."[2] And the psychologist Michael F. Andrews adds, "Creativity is an expression of one's uniqueness. To be creative, then, is to be oneself."[3]

• Have a self-image that says you are creative. This can be helped if you liberate yourself from close identification with "I am what I do." Any particular roles you play in life—engineer, housewife, professor, manager, student, and so forth—imply certain expectations and responsibilities that hamper your creative powers when seeking original solutions to the problems you encounter. The moment you transcend the "I am what I do" and become "I am I," you become more open to unique and fresh insights from your unconscious.

## SPECIFIC PREPARATION
## FOR CREATIVE PROBLEM SOLVING

The deeper a person's understanding of his problem, the better he is able to marshal a multitude of approaches and methods when tackling them. To increase your understanding of your problems, do the following:

• Read widely and examine the literature with both a critical and an imaginative attitude. Be aware that what you read is not necessarily the last word on the subject, nor is it always the best possible position established. Findings and facts are fluid and dynamic, and they change all the time. In order to find out more about your problem, deliberately assume that the important facts are, as yet, not known and that you will have to discover them. Question even the most authoritative sources on the problem and note by what procedures the "facts" were established.

• Sift fact from opinion or assumption, but be generous toward ideas that seem to you unorthodox or unusual. Instead of proceeding to demonstrate how untenable they are, imagine what would happen if these ideas were really true.

• Once you have formulated your problem, seek out all available sources of information on it. Become saturated with pertinent knowledge and data. However, at the same time critically examine the most time-honored, taken-for-granted aspects of this problem. Are they still valid or true? Look for the key factors of your problem and try to isolate them. Make personal observations and experiments. Remember that lack of thorough analysis of your problem may often cost you invaluable hours spent on a wrong problem or on a side issue not really relevant to your problem. Don't be discouraged in advance because others who have tried to solve the same problem have failed. Remember that conditions change, and what did not work once might work now.

• If your problem requires further study and the mastery of new knowledge or techniques, don't discard the problem, but proceed to put in as much effort as you can in learning the requisite materials to achieve the solution. The rewards of a creative solution far exceed the effort and perseverance put into it.

## THE PROBLEM APPROACH

Almost everyone these days is, as a rule, besieged by problems, so the question "Where does one find problems?" should not preoccupy us much. Those individuals who are not able to spot problems can best develop or stimulate their sensitivity to potential improvements by starting to ask themselves questions: "What am I doing, or what is done that could be done more effectively, better, cheaper, differently?" Sometimes the negative approach, "What's wrong with this?" will furnish a list of irritants that can provide a source of problems.

Because of the tremendous number of problems that are thrust upon us in every realm of activity, our real difficulty often is to spot the *real* or *important* problem. Therefore it is advisable to arrange problems hierarchically in terms of their importance, difficulty, and feasibility of possible solution. You should first make a list of problems to be solved and then proceed to pick out for special attention those problems that combine your optimum interest and understanding with the importance of the problem.

## HOW TO DEFINE THE PROBLEM

The next step in the procedure is to define the problem, based on your understanding of it. Correct problem definition, or statement, is crucial to effective solutions. Incorrect problem definition frequently ties you down to a restrictive error, which prevents effective solutions. Fluency of ideas and flexibility of thought are likewise affected by incorrect problem statements. Consequently, the first problem definitions should be considered tentative. You might have to modify or expand the meaning of your initial definition several times. Occasionally additional data must be first collected in order to define the problem at all.

- State your problem in a simple, basic, broad, generic way, so that it does not limit or confine your thinking. Do not structure your problem statement too much.

- Strip from it all side problems or conditions and as many modifying adjectives, adverbs, and phrases as possible.

- Take care that you do not suggest a solution in your problem definition. Look beyond the immediate problem to its fundamentals.

- Keep asking yourself: "What are the actual boundaries of the problem?" and "What are the unusual aspects of the problem, those that everybody takes for granted, and can they really be taken for granted?"

- See if you can't state your problem in a different way. Remember that creative problems have several acceptable or "right" solutions, unlike analytical problems, which have only one right answer. Listing variations of the problem statement may even sometimes suggest the idea for solution.

- Break down the parameters or variables of the problem through analysis, at the same time keeping in your mind's eye the total problem situation and the proper relationship of the parts of the whole. Organize the facts pertaining to your problem italicizing your key facts.

After the problem is defined:

- Prepare yourself a problem sheet on which you write down your problem statement(s). Check it critically for clarity, accuracy, and completeness. If unsure about the clarity of meaning, check it with your colleagues.

- Next list the ideas and various approaches that you feel might conceivable solve the problem. Take off in different directions, and amass as many leads as you can. Note down all the ideas, even the insignificant ones, but abstain from dwelling upon any single one of them for too long during this process. Also, do not follow only one line of thought at this point, for this would prevent others from occurring. Even if you feel that you have hit upon one idea that looks to you as the best answer to your problem, resist the impulse to stop the process. Write it down so it will not be lost. Many fleeting thoughts, which, in isolation, may appear inconsequential, may contain a new vital germ of an idea, or later, in combination with other thoughts, may combine into a new, meaningful idea. Remember that no idea should be rejected at this stage as being of no consequence until later proven so.

• Another thing to avoid when the creative current is running strong is referring to any great extent to the literature for data. Cursory checking of facts is all right, but extensive literature searches at this time can completely divert you from your original line of thought.

• Exhaust all the possible and conceivable hypotheses and plans for action. Consider even the most unlikely solutions. List the many specific methods that you could conceivably use to approach the problem solution. But refrain from evaluating any of the suggestions and hunches that occur to you at this time.

• Look for analogous situations in other areas, at the same time remembering that none will fit your problem precisely.

• Relax your binding faith in reason and logic when creating ideas, and let your imagination soar.

• Refuse to be downed by failure. Continue working at your problem in the face of any serious discouragement you might feel, and resist the temptation to give up. Patience and perseverance are two of the most valuable assets in creative problem solving. Most highly creative individuals were willing to try again and again, in spite of serious discouragement, and thus overcame many failures before they achieved success.

• Do not be disturbed if you experience a sense of stress when looking for a solution. Without this feeling, you run the risk of not finding the best solution. Have faith in yourself and believe that the answer will come.

• Sustained creative thinking, when the problem is tackled from every conceivable angle, will usually yield enough material for you to put it into a systematic, orderly outline. Frequently, to your surprise, you may have come up with many more ideas than you thought you would be capable of producing. Even if no satisfactory solution emerges at this time, the unremitting, sustained concentration leaves your unconscious with a wealth of material to work on, and, after a few days away from a problem, when you renew attacking it, you may find that you are more productive than during your previous concentration on the problem. "Sleeping on the problem" has proven extremely valuable by almost all creative people. But it is always preceded by the intense preliminary spadework of analysis.

• The next time you tackle your problem again, go over the ideas you had previously listed. Try various combinations of them. Often one idea will start you off on a completely new direction. This time follow it freely, even though it may seem to you that the new train of thought takes you off your immediate concern in the problem area.

• If you still do not make any progress toward a solution, reexamine your problem with reference to the problem definition(s). Is it too broad, preventing anchorage points? Is it too limited, narrowing your field of thought? Should you divide your problem into several subproblems and work on them one at a time? In any case, the previous efforts at analysis and definition have given you a better understanding of your problem, and now, after you have redefined it, you may be on the last lap of a determined surge toward solution.


## STIMULATING THE CREATIVE PROCESS

In order to increase your powers of observation and association during creative problem solving:

• Suspend critical thinking when thinking creatively—learn to turn your judgment on and off at will. During the heat of creative problem solving, criticism and judgment must be suspended. Once you have learned how to defer judgment, you are capable of producing ideas in quantity; and quantity, like free association, taps the unconscious sources of creativity and leads to originality and quality. It is speculated that Sigmund Freud developed his basic therapeutic modality of free-association as a result of reading an essay by journalist Ludwig Borne. This essay, written in 1823, entitled "The Art of Becoming an Original Writer in Three Days," recommends the following:

> Here follows the practical prescription I promised. Take a few sheets of paper and for three days in succession write down, without any falsification or hypocrisy, everything that comes into your head. Write what you think of yourself, of your women, of the Turkish war, of Goethe, of the Fonk criminal case, of the Last Judgment, of those senior to you in authority—and when the three days are over you will be amazed at what novel and startling thoughts have welled up in you.[4]

• Try setting idea quotas for yourself. But set yourself realistic deadlines. Do not give up if ideas are slow in coming. When you set yourself idea quotas, be sure that your time is not too strictly limited. A sense of leisure and a sense of freedom from time restrictions are important factors in the solution of problems.

• Always carry a notebook with you. Ideas strike at any hour and under the strangest of circumstances. If you fail to make a notation of them, they may disappear back into the unconscious. Do not trust your memory. We often let a good idea slip away from us because we think we will remember it afterward. More often than not, however, an idea that occurs to us during a brief moment is irretrievably lost if not recorded on the spot.

• Orderliness applies also to creative thinking. Plan your steps, keep records, and cultivate proper habits.

• Regularly schedule practice and development efforts to improve your facility for grouping knowledge into new combinations.

• Proper mood is important for creative work, but the best method is not to wait for it, but to pick up the pencil and start writing down the different parts of your problem, the different approaches you might use, and the directions you might want to explore. As appetite comes by eating, so creative mood will come when you are actively engaged in the exercise of writing things down.

• Sometimes the effort or ritual of preparing for work may be effective in producing the proper mood or emotional tone. You should deliberately perform such acts that create the atmosphere for your best creative thinking.

• During the creative process you should practice *empathic involvement;* that is, you should attempt to *feel* the ramifications of your problem. You should, in a sense, imaginatively become the thing you are creating or the problem you are solving. After a period of involvement you should detach yourself from the problem and view it objectively from a distance. Effective creative process requires continuous shifting between involvement and detachment.

• If you are not making any headway, even after your "second wind," drop your problem completely and do something entirely different. Break off and relax. Unremitting pressure sometimes interferes with the unconscious formation of new configurations. Organize your time so that you can have long periods when you can engage in hobbies or be completely alone and silent. Make a game of the images that come to you during the periods of relaxation. Remember that creative insight occurs most often in relaxed or dispersed attention. The *closure* appears frequently after you have left the problem in despondency or disgust.

• For proper assimilation of experiences, you should allow a certain amount of time in your daily activities for solitude and meditation. A daily schedule which does not allow for solitary absorption, sorting and reshaping of information and experience, works as an effective barrier to the emergence of rewarding creative ideas.

• Sometimes it is not advisable to discuss your ideas with others during their preliminary stages, before you have developed and crystallized them to some degree. A discussion too early in the process might make your idea disappear into thin air, or it might give you false leads or change your original mode of approach. It might also abate the driving power behind your motivation. On the other hand, meeting with congenial people who work in the same problem area may give you additional enthusiasm to continue with your work. There are no hard-and-fast rules here. You have to discover for yourself whether initial discussion helps or hinders you. Sometimes discussing your problem with people who have never done any work in your field can give you a new slant on the problem. Such people have a fresh, naive point of view, and in the process of explaining your problem to them you are often made aware of certain obscurities or incongruities in your approach that you may have overlooked before. Also, naive questions surprisingly often help to arrive at a refreshing, new viewpoint.

• A few times in your life you may be lucky to have a so-called "avalanche experience," when ideas come in a flood after a major solution to a difficult problem. One idea seems to spark the development of others and these in turn again others. Many of the ideas are related ideas, but even dissimilar germinal ideas do occur during this period. Failing to record them promptly may cost you months or even years of fruitful ideas.

• Determine the physical conditions during which you regularly do your best work. If you find out, for example, that certain physical postures, for example, pacing the floor, sitting quietly at your desk, lying down or relaxing in an easy chair, are conducive to your best work, you should not hesitate to use them. In fact, you should deliberately make an effort to ascertain what sort of physical activity accompanies your most productive efforts, and then deliberately assume it when attempting to solve your problems. Avoid distractions and intrusions as much as possible. Choose a time when you can stay with your problem hours on end without interruptions from others.

• Develop a *retrospective awareness* of the periods when you solved your problems creatively. Note the methods that were successful and those that failed. Try to retrace and rehearse the routes that were successful.

• Schedule your creative problem-solving periods for those times when you have your most favorable mental set for creative work.

• Be prepared and alert for the "moment of surprise." Be alert for ideas when riding in a car or train, while at the movies or at the concert, and especially during the brief periods preceding and following sleep. It is incredible how many insights all of us fail to record and utilize because they take us by surprise or because of our lack of courage or temporary diffidence.


## EVALUATING THE IDEA

Although this section and the next, "How to Present the Idea," are fully discussed in my book, *How to Sell New Ideas,* a few relevant points have been included here.

Before you are ready to present your idea to others, you should closely evaluate it along the following points:

• The time it takes to put it into shape so it can be worked out in a concrete form.

• How valuable will it be? What about its timeliness and practical aspects? What about the extent of improvement it promises over existing things? What about its breadth of applications?

• What about its sales appeal? Does it fill a real need or does the need have to be created through promotional and advertising efforts? How ready is the market for it? Have the possible user criticisms or difficulties been foreseen?

• What eventual savings will this new idea realize? What about the materials to be used in the production of this new device or process? Have the possible constructional, design, and manufacturing difficulties or objections been considered?

• Is it compatible with other company activities and production?

• Does the company have the necessary equipment and manpower to produce the item? What costs would be involved in getting the special equipment and recruiting the necessary manpower, if needed?

• Has the operational soundness of the idea been reviewed and checked in all its ramifications? What about any possible technical faults or limitations of the idea?

• Is it possible to work out several variations of the idea so management can exercise choice in selecting the commercially most promising type?

• What about your position in the company? Does it reduce or enhance the acceptance of the idea you will propose?

• Before you present your idea, it would be advisable if you asked your close associates for their frank comments. If anyone criticizes your idea, you should show tolerance and understanding and study the objections dispassionately and objectively. You should remove the possible "bugs" that others may have pointed out. If, after keen analysis of the objections, you are still convinced that your idea is as sound and promising as you can make it, you are ready to prepare for the presentation of the idea. To reduce the chances of rejection, you should put as much thought and effort into preparing your presentation as you did in developing the idea.

## HOW TO PRESENT THE IDEA

Presenting a new idea is in many ways one of the most crucial aspects of the entire creative process. It is at this stage that many a brilliant idea dies stillborn because the creative individual fails to communicate the brainchild persuasively to others. In order to augment the chances of success, the following guideposts should be heeded and followed with fidelity:

- In most companies, the immediate manager or supervisor is the first person to sell on the new idea. Once you get his or her backing, selling the idea to management then becomes a much easier task.

- If you have to present the idea to a group or a committee, prior to the meeting, you should first try to sell your idea to one or two members of the group. These individuals often appreciate this advance confidence shown in them and will rally to your side if and when the going gets rough during the presentation.

- Before the actual presentation of the idea, you should give a short background history of the problem, telling what led you to investigate the area in the first place and how you then proceeded to solve the problem.

- You should not get overly anxious and anticipate rejection, because this will spoil your manner of presentation. On the other hand, you should be prepared to answer all possible questions, to give all the data and facts pertaining to the idea, and to explain what reasoning you used to arrive at the new idea.

- The presentation should be made as concise and to the point as feasible. Supervisors and managers are busy people, and they may get impatient with long-winded preliminaries and side issues. You have to be sure, however, that you cover all the pertinent facts.

• When your audience includes one or more highly sophisticated people, you have to include all possible counterarguments opposed to your idea and discuss these also. This two-sided approach will help you to convince the more sophisticated persons of the thoroughness that went into the conception and execution of the idea. With analytically sophisticated people, the prime requirement is to be thorough, but not necessarily brief.

• The new material should be presented no faster than it can be understood and absorbed. Clear and lucid language and terminology that is within the grasp of the listeners should be used.

• Arguments to any possible objections or criticisms should be well prepared, but you would be well advised not to articulate them before they are actually needed. An argumentative approach in presentation creates the impression of unnecessary defensiveness. An overly argumentative approach may also change the entire atmosphere or attitudes of the people listening to you.

• Special attention has to be paid to the practical details of the idea—how it can be executed and implemented. The advantages as well as the costs and difficulties involved should be pointed out. Nothing kills the chances of a new idea faster than a purely technical or abstract way of presenting it. When selling the idea to management, it should be remembered that a strong dollars-and-cents orientation has to be met. The possible sales appeals and profit potentials should definitely be demonstrated, and the presentation should include plenty of "benefits to us" statements and not solely dwell on the "how it works" kind of discourse.

• Be prepared for all questions concerning the implementation of the idea. Also make sure you know what your firm's competition may be doing in this area. Point out what real need your idea fills, what concrete benefits its has. You can never take it for granted that management is familiar with the need or its importance.

• People are, as a rule, notoriously poor visualizers. Therefore, whenever possible, it behooves you to augment your verbal description with the aid of suitable sketches, charts, or even actual models that the group can touch and handle. Mere verbal description overly taxes attention and, especially with new ideas, often lacks clarity. Communicating a new idea requires co-creation on the part of the listeners, and they have to get a clear idea and perspective about what would happen if the proposed idea is adopted.

• When you present your idea, be aware that your reputation and good judgment will be put to the acid test. If your idea or presentation is inadequate, it will reflect upon your future status in the company and make selling any future ideas even more difficult. The image management has of you is highly important in getting your idea accepted. If you have a previous reputation for trustworthiness and experience, the easier it will be for you to sell them on your idea.

• Overselling should be avoided. While enthusiasm has a contagious quality, a superabundance of it, especially at the beginning of the presentation when the full story still has to be told, will put people on the defensive, and they may not give the idea the consideration it warrants.

• When arguments against the idea are raised, it is frequently advisable not to attempt an immediate refutation unless you are sure it is absolutely convincing. Often it is more advisable to follow the unrefuted argument up with another very positive argument in the idea's favor. Later, when a more positive tone of the session has been built up again, the unrefuted argument may be taken up and effectively neutralized in a few declarative and positive statement.

• If the idea is too radical or too big it should be presented piecemeal, in logical order and sequence. This prepares the group gradually for the acceptance of the entire new idea.

• You should never assume an air of superiority when presenting your idea, nor show any excess pride of paternity. This may make the other persons in the group feel small or inferior, and the negative emotional climate that is evoked acts as a strong resistance to the new suggestions even before the presentation is completed.

• In cases when the investigation of a problem has previously been approved by management, you have already won half the battle, and selling the new approach you have invented should be much easier.

• If you are not sure of the accuracy of your statements when answering questions, do not try to hide this, but state that you will find out the exact answer and pass it on to the questioner later.

- It will help a great deal if you know as much as possible about the people to whom you have to present your idea—their temperaments, aptitudes, idiosyncracies, and preferences. Knowing their characteristics will enable you to so formulate your presentation as to measurably increase the probability of acceptance.

- You should learn to write effective reports, for, no matter how brilliant your idea, an inability to describe it effectively in written form may reduce its chances of acceptance.

- You should leave copies of your report with the people who listened to the presentation. They may want to study it more afterward.

- At the end of your presentation, you should sum up the more salient points you have made, the anticipated benefits and advantages of the idea, and why you think the idea should be implemented forthright.

## REFERENCES

[1] Chester I. Barnard, *The Functions of the Executive*. (Cambridge, Mass.: Harvard University Press, 1946), dedication page.

[2] Clark E. Moustakas, *Creative Life*. (New York: Van Nostrand Reinhold Company, 1977), p. 25.

[3] Michael F. Andrews, "The Dialectics of Creativity and Mental Health," in *Creativity and Psychological Health*, ed., Michael F. Andrews (Syracuse, N.Y.: Syracuse University Press, 1961), p. 95.

[4] Frederic F. Flach, *Choices*. (Philadelphia: J.B. Lippincott Company, 1977), pp. 138–39.

# INDEX